Growin' up in Lancashire

GROWIN' UP IN LANCASHIRE

MEMORIES OF A NORTHERN CHILDHOOD

Written by Brian Carline

Illustrated by David Summerville

For Auntie Minnie, Uncle John and Auntie Doreen
whose kindness and generosity over the years
is much appreciated

First published in 2014
by Palatine Books,
Carnegie House,
Chatsworth Road
Lancaster LA1 4SL
www.palatinebooks.com

British Library Cataloguing-in-Publication data
A catalogue record for this book is available from the British Library

ISBN 13: 978-1-874181-99-6

Designed and typeset by Carnegie Book Production

www.carnegiebookproduction.com
Printed and bound by Page Bros Ltd

Contents

Introduction

THIS WAS 1956 AND HERBIE would do anything for a dare. You know, outrageous and crazy things. Describing him as 'gormless' I thought was an understatement; 'nutter' was probably a more appropriate label. I'd seen this nine-year-old kid narrowly escape death from a steam train as he retrieved bits of coal from the railway track. I'd also witnessed him running across the asbestos roof of a factory, only to disappear into the workshop below as it cracked under his weight. Herbie was my best mate.

Another life threatening experience involving Herbie happened when he let loose a barrage of stones at a large nest of wasps under the eaves of Pendleton church. Herbie quickly gained 'first-hand' experience as to the social behaviour of these creatures. Realising he had upset them, he shot off at high speed, pursued by several thousand of the angry insects. The chase came to an end on Broad Street outside *The Helping Hand Clothing Company*, with Herbie now stuffed with more venom than a Portuguese Man o'War. His mother, skilled in dealing with such medical emergencies, filled the galvanised washtub with water and plunged him in below the water line. Her home remedy for dealing with this kind of trauma was to chuck in a couple of Dolly Blue bags for good measure. The chemistry of these washing aids took away the pain of the stings and its ultra-marine blue made his shirt collar the whitest it had ever been.

One final example of Herbie's apparent desire not to make the age of ten was when local bully Rita Golightly called him chicken. To prove to her that he was as fearless as Dick Barton, my mate Herbie rose to the bait by consuming three boxes of Imps lozenges, one after another. There must have been a hundred of these liquorice pellets in each box. To this day, I have never observed such a dramatic change in a person. He opened his mouth to reveal teeth as black as a sack of nutty slack. His inky tongue waved around like a probing leech and his lips resembled those of a moribund soul soon to depart from this world.

There was, however, a side effect for which Herbie hadn't bargained. The liquorice and menthol diamond-shaped sweets not only raised the temperature of his mouth, but consumed in such excess they caused severe bloating. Aftwer a couple of hours, this usually skinny urchin took on the shape and size of a hot air balloon. His new corpulence, coupled with the drastic change in the colour of his complexion, forced his mother to give him a clout round the ear and then cart him off to hospital. There he remained for five days, baffling physicians, who had to admit that they had never before come across anyone quite like Herbie.

* * *

In the forties and fifties, if your house possessed an outside loo or a 'bucket and chuck it' at the bottom of the garden, then a visit on a freezing winter's day could be a hypothermic experience. My gran once described a sub zero session out there as being 'Cold enough for two hairnets', so you did what you had to do extremely quickly. But to add insult to injury, even the briefest time on the pan could be made even less comfortable by the dreaded Izal toilet paper. I had seen adverts in the *Daily Sketch* for this stuff. The propaganda pictured a mother cuddling and reassuring her two children. The caption read 'Mum Knows Best – Use Izal Medicated Toilet Paper'. The material had been sprayed with disinfectant and hence branded 'medicated'.

Usually we had the luxury of cut up squares of the *Daily Mirror*, and my gran thoughtfully advised us never to use pieces of glossy periodicals after some bloke in the next street once used a large shiny magazine picture of Sophia Loren to solve his needs and unexpectedly lacerated his anus on the staples.

At school we were familiar with Izal and printed on it were the words 'Now Wash Your Hands.' This was sensible advice, for these wipes had the absorbency of a roof tile, and as my uncle Cyril would say, 'It just seems to move stuff around.' Using Izal, you took the rough with the smooth, for each sheet possessed a shiny side and a coarse, matt finish on the other. My mum knew someone who worked in Salford's dole office and she would pinch packets of this paper and give some to us. This meant that, after we had completed our mission and risen from the throne, the warning 'Government Property' appeared imprinted on our rears. A non-medicated rival of Izal was Bronco, aptly named because it too gave you a rough ride.

Many of us children knew this material was also great for making comb and paper kazoos, while its unique composition beat mum's greaseproof paper hands down as tracing paper. This was because Izal's coarse side helpfully gripped the page and refused to slide about. Some thirty years later, as a young teacher, I received an absence note from a pupil which read, 'My son Gary was not in school yesterday 'cos he was suffering from dyor [crossed out], dyeeyer [crossed out], dyar [crossed out] ... the trots.' This correspondence made me feel extremely uneasy because it was written on a sheet of Izal toilet paper!

Izal, then, was iconic. Of its time. Recalling it brings memories for me of growing up in Lancashire in the '40s and '50s flooding back, and it represents the aim of this book: to recall and reminisce about all the things that were part of our childhood. Dinky toys, skipping ropes made from clothes line, bagatelle, dolly tubs and lucky bags. They were times when you as kids spent most of your playtime outdoors in areas designated as 'Play Streets' where games you played such as 'IT', hopscotch, five stones and football, could take place in safety. You participated in villainous games such as 'Knock Down Ginger' or 'Robber's Knock', where you knocked on someone's door and then ran away. I believe it is still played today but they now call it 'Parcel Force'.

If you can remember things about your kitchen such as Echo margarine, pink carbolic soap and an old jam jar where you'd keep the rent money, then you were as poor as we were. The carbolic soap would appear on a Sunday night, which was always designated as 'bath night'. The galvanised bath would be placed on the rag rug in front of the fire and then topped up with kettles full of water or water straight from 'the copper'. There was a strict order of bathing in our house. In first was my mother, followed by us kids, then the whippets and finally my gran. By that time the carbolic had killed everything in the water with which it came into contact, ranging from bacteria to whippets. My mother would place a brick under one end of the bath, creating a deep and shallow end. My older brothers sat in the deep water whilst I clung onto the sides of the elevated section with my bottom stuck against the bath's hard, rough base.

Out on the highway in these times dogs would chase cars, and Humber Hawks outpaced Austin A35s. Arriving at some destination on a motorcycle and sidecar gave you little cachet and made it impossible for you to look cool and dignified. Ice cream was dispensed from carts pulled by a horse. Rag and Bone men gave you donkey stones to brighten your doorstep in exchange for old bedsteads and clothes. In these times there was an obsession with corporate uniforms. They were worn by employees ranging from milkmen to park keepers. Postmen wore proper livery and did not pose around in shorts as they do today. Hospital doctors wore white coats. Little girls clad themselves in their mother's dresses and shuffled along pavements in high heels and smeared in lipstick. Boys played 'Japs and Commandos' on bombsites whilst grans were busy knitting woollen bathing costumes and balaclavas. People stood for the national anthem at the end of an evening at the cinema and Fess Parker *was* king of the wild frontier.

If nostalgia of this kind means something to you, whether your memory lane was cobbled and lined with identical terraced houses or was rather more fancy, then please read on. Many of us remember those as hard times that bred a resilience and strength of character. To us youngsters who played in these streets, they were good and happy times. They were, indeed, the days of Growin' up in Lancashire.

Brian Carline

January 2014

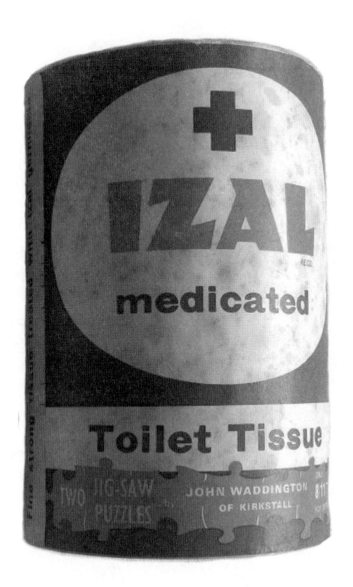

Dyb, dyb, dyb, dob, dob, dob

WALTER KIPPLE WAS A COLOURLESS LAD. In fact, I'd say there was more substance in a glass of water. His physical appearance too suggested he was an embryonic afterthought. There was nothing about his morphology that was fine-tuned. Walter had prominent teeth to such a degree that whenever his mouth closed they would remain on show like the keys on a piano. His National Health Service spectacles were held in place on his nose by a piece of knicker elastic, stretched around the back of his head. I suppose today we would know this ingenious support as Spec Savers. A grubby, all weather plaster was taped across one of its lenses to remedy his squint. Walter's ophthalmic problem was so severe that on the odd occasion he removed his specs, he could look fifteen people in the eye, all at once.

Walter's mother, anxious for him to cope with the transitions of puberty, encouraged him to join the cub scouts and subsequently enrolled him in the First Pendleton cubs that met on Tuesday evenings at Brunswick Methodist church. Baden-Powell, the founder of this illustrious movement, would have celebrated Walter's undying allegiance to the cub scout movement. Its motto, 'Be Prepared', led Walter to always carry a spare length of this elastic in case the current piece broke.

There were twelve of us lads – well, thirteen if you counted Terry Corless. Terry suffered from alarming bouts of asthma and was a poor attender. Living next to Greengate and Irwell rubber works did him no favours. His permanently blue lips made him look as though he had been sucking liquorice sticks. Games of blow football, played with drinking straws were beyond his capabilities, along with whistling and blowing out his own birthday candles.

The nickname for our troop should have been the dirty dozen. Although passing your Tenderpad induction into the Wolf Cubs required a certain standard of personal cleanliness, most of the bunch sported engrained tide-marks that would have competed with a bag of John Innes compost. There was, however, one exception. Giles Barraclough had a cherubic air about him. Indeed this aura was a curious mixture of pink carbolic and TCP. There were certainly no germs on Giles. His mother, deemed by many as living above her station, in reality lived above Whitehead's Cobblers in two rooms with a shared WC. Mrs Barraclough would boast they lived in a detached property. It wasn't; the premises were coming away from the rest of the shops due to mining subsidence. Should people ever inquire as to what she was having for tea, she would reply with the soft, yet eloquent air of a Sloane Square sophisticate, 'Lancashire calamari à l'oignon' – tripe and onions to you and me.

Because times were hard, none of us could afford the complete cub uniform. Benny Benson wore his brother's large school cap, which swamped his head, and when he spoke you wondered where the noise was coming from. Philip Townley had a bulldog clip for a woggle and Sandy Krink's jersey was a red polo-neck rather than the V-neck cub standard issue green. Perhaps most worrying of all was Giles's neckerchief, which was his mum's shiny green silk, paisley design scarf. He also wore blindingly clean patent leather sandals and had Giles ever said he was off camping, he might well have been misunderstood!

Garters for socks really meant rubber bands and our Akela pinched loads of them from his workplace at The Times Furnishing Company. George Marshall, born in Baguley (pronounced Bagley – the letter 'u' can't be arsed), was Akela of this Pendleton pack. At the start of every meeting we had to line up and George would spray us with carbolic he'd poured into an old Flit fly spray pump. George always seemed to regard us as contaminated and this preventative medicine was his way of maintaining aseptic conditions for the evening. In a way I could understand his mania. Terry always had some rash, Royston suffered from itinerant boils and Henry would constantly smell of unwanted material.

Following our dousing with carbolic and Flit we were instructed to gather in a circle and to endure the grand howl. At the age of nine, I found this futile ritual a tad over the top. The only good thing in this tedious ceremony of wolf cub loyalty was Royston Birtwistle who would offer V signs to Akela's back rather than the prescribed closed two-fingered scout salute.

The term raggy arsed could also have described our unit. Short trousers bore tears, patches and stains lashed into place somewhere around the waist by snake belts or braces. There was something odd about the elasticity of Royston's braces. His short, grey trousers were his brother's cast offs and far too big for him. Consequently, whenever he walked or ran, the said pants would oscillate up and down revealing knees, then no knees. The trouser movements finally halted a good fifteen seconds after his body movements had ceased.

When I joined the wolf cub pack I heard the other boys calling George 'Akela'. In the North West we refer to people of the same family or fraternity as 'our'. My brother was 'our Peter' or more commonly referred to as 'our kid'. Subsequently, for a number of weeks many of the new recruits believed George's first name to be Calar or Kaylar, and that he was, to us boys, 'Our Kaylar'. Come to think of it, intelligence of this standard meant that a large number of the pack failed the eleven plus.

George was ancient, about mid forties. He was always immaculately presented in full scout uniform. Khaki shirt and shorts, a polished woggle, knee-length socks turned down at the knee with green tabbed garters. His brown, sensible shoes were always highly polished. He had more badges on his shirt than fabric and always round his neck, lying on top of his green and yellow neckerchief, was an old ARP whistle attached to a piece of string. The item of real envy, however, was attached to his brown trouser belt: a six-inch Bowie knife. Royston Birtwistle often played at being Akela and shoved his mum's bread knife through his snake belt. The knife was used to whittle wood and also to play the dangerous game of Split the Kipper. The sport was played on soft ground and involved throwing a knife some distance away from your opponent's feet. Should the knife stick into the ground the opponent had to span that distance with his legs. Tragedy forced Walter's mum to put an end to such an irresponsible and downright alarming game when Royston's blade got stuck in Walter's foot. The pastime still continued but was then renamed by us insensitive urchins as Split the Kipple.

I would often stare at George's knees. The term knobbly totally failed to do them justice. Indeed, his knees gave the impression that he was storing ball bearings under his skin. A few inches above this dreadful part of his anatomy was hair, but hair on a grand scale. It was hair only to be found elsewhere in nature on the Dulux dog. We reckoned George must comb his legs, he had so much of it. To complete his authority George had difficulty pronouncing Rs. Consequently when he taught us the cub scout law, his version was:

'I pwomise to do my best. I can be twusted. A cub scout is fwendly and weliable and considewate.'

It just didn't quite give him the macho edge he might have wanted.

Another member of this disparate bunch of loyalists was Henry Delaney. Whether it was a scorching ninety degrees in the shade or a Winter's blizzard registering off the Beaufort Scale, Henry would wear his balaclava. When questioned about its permanent appearance on his head, he would reply,

"Cos I gorra weak chest and me mam told me I gorra wear it!'

Now, you didn't argue with Mrs Delaney. Mr Delaney certainly didn't and neither would have Rommel. She could undo knots in lorry ropes with her teeth, and was the kind of woman you would not feel comfortable about asking round for afternoon tea. She may well have had a penchant for rope but where knitting was concerned, I am afraid the laws of knit one, purl one eluded her. Henry's balaclava possessed no symmetry whatsoever and the mandatory holes for Henry to both breathe and see were all over the place. My mum said Henry's balaclava resembled the vote of a parliamentary debate – eyes to the right and nose to the left.

To promote an *esprit de corps*, Akela would encourage us to go for badges and stars. We all enjoyed bandaging people and lighting fires but learning about how to tell if the Union Jack was the right way up or growing mustard and cress seeds was boring. Knot tying was an acceptable experience but open to abuse as weaker members of the pack were tied to the church railings. Giles and Walter were the usual casualties of sheepshanks and reef knots. Akela got into trouble from Mrs Kipple one cold December evening. She accused him of not supervising his group. Three of us had tied her beloved offspring upside down onto the church notice board. The inverted figure of Walter hung there moaning, suspended by square knots and clove hitches. Across the top of the notice board, just above Walter's feet was this week's church message. It read, 'See what Jesus can do for you.'

To get our 'Leaping Wolf' badge, each one of us had to undertake a personal challenge. These would range from swimming a length of Pendleton baths under water to walking to Bury and back. The School Board man set Dougie Broadbent's personal challenge. He insisted that Dougie should attend school and not work on the market with his dad. Giles was particularly good hearted, always helping old ladies across the road, even when they were happily seated in their living rooms.

Akela seemed obsessed with us being able to save lives. The number of times he shouted at us, 'A cub scout pwomises to do his best. To do his duty to God and the Queen and to help other people!'

Helping other people, in George's eyes, included bandaging them up and dragging them on a stretcher to safety. One particular evening we were learning how to immobilise an injured soul on a small scaffold board. Tony Sutcliffe was the moribund patient and was quickly lashed to the board complete with head bandage and splints to his legs. George now suggested we should learn how to transport the casualty over high ground: the six-foot brick boundary wall of the church would suffice. Four of us stood on top of this structure and were proceeding to haul him up and over. Seconds before we reached the summit, Mrs Sutcliffe entered the yard carrying a tray of treacle toffee.

'I'll put it down here for you boys. Help yourself!' she shouted. Generosity of this magnitude demanded an instant response, so we dropped the ropes from which her son was suspended and jumped down to feed on such scrumptious delights. Tony's descent was rapid. He fell six foot in under one second, completely obeying Newton's laws of motion. The ambulance crew that took Tony off to hospital praised us for the first aid we had administered. George never told them that the first aid had been given in advance of the trauma. The four of us who were responsible for Tony's fortnight in hospital each received a bad conduct badge, which then seemed to neutralise the good conduct badges we had earned the previous week for rescuing Mrs Serafinowicz's cat from a grid in the street. Mind you, we put it there in the first place.

As we approached the age when we were eligible for enrolment into the scouts, we were exposed to more challenging experiences and tests. Den-making proved popular but Reverend Smallpeace protested at us removing half of his privet bushes to make a bivouac. I never knew a servant of God knew so many bad words. Some of them I'd heard my mate Herbie's dad say when he was displeased about things. I feel he should have appreciated that this was the urban landscape of Salford, and woodland was in short supply.

Sleeping outdoors involved us bedding down in the church yard. This experience was nothing new to Gordon Simmister. His family were always doing moonlight flits and we reckoned that the Simmisters saw more darkness than daylight. The Birtwistles had been evicted five times to my knowledge and so Royston was also familiar with al fresco life. Mind you, our house roof leaked water like the Trevi fountain, so getting a bit wet on a September dawn was nothing new to me either.

Physical recreation formed a major part of our wolf cub life. Most sessions finished in playing British Bulldog, which was really open season for beating up the likes of Walter and Giles. It was bullying and psychopathy in its broadest sense and George was never much use at controlling this physical game. It usually ended in someone being flattened and in tears. One of the tests for securing your first star was the ability to turn a somersault – a painful experience on the gnarled floorboards of the church hall. Another was to be able to leap frog over another cub; no problem if you chose Walter. However, if Sandy Krink bent over it was like staring at a Saxon tumulus and the leap usually ended in bruises for both parties.

Once a month our pack, along with the scouts, had to attend church parade. Most of our outfit were pagans or orthodox 'couldn't give a bugger'. It was usually George, Giles, Walter and myself who represented the First Pendleton cubs. I was brought up a good, Catholic lad and my gran was unhappy about me compromising my faith for wolf cub status. I really don't know what she was moaning about when she said God would punish me for this betrayal. At both Catholic and Methodist services we sang the hymn, 'The Lord is my shepherd, I shall not want'. Shall not want? Shall not want? You try telling that to the Anderton family next door to us, when the bedding and Mrs Anderton's wedding ring had to go into pawn to see them through the rest of the week. Rather short-sighted of God, I thought.

There was rejoicing and anticipation when Salford Council announced that the Queen would be visiting parts of the North West, which included a trip through Salford. Her route would be along Broad Street where crowds could gather to cheer and wish her well. George went into panic mode when he was instructed to provide a patriotic, flag-waving contingent of boy scouts and wolf cubs near to Pendleton church. The problem for George was that nobody in our pack had the full uniform. At best, we resembled a bunch of Dickensian waifs. Mrs Lomas called our unit The Crazy Gang and said we looked like refugees escaping from the Russian front. George only managed to place three of us in the front line who were completely attired to do the flag waving. The likes of Sandy Krink with his fiery red sweater and Henry Delaney in his black balaclava that made him look like a paediatric terrorist, were both banished to three rows back. Tony Sutcliffe looked smart in his full cub regalia but couldn't wave his flag as he was still on crutches and recovering from the mountain rescue debacle two months earlier.

My only sight of Her Majesty was when her huge, black limousine sped past us doing at least thirty miles an hour. All I could see was a pink blur and some white gloves waving away.

The ever pragmatic Ena Lomas instantly assessed the situation.

'I expect she was wantin' her tea,' was her analysis.

'Is thar it!' shouted an aggrieved Royston. 'I had a wash for that?'

'I could see sod all!' barked a disappointed Benny Benson.

'I'm not surprised in that cap, Benny,' called Terry Corless who, today, looked less blue than normal.

In 1949, the concept of 'Bob A Job' week came into being, fully endorsed by the Boy Scout executive. In 1990 the last job was done and the practice was abandoned for health and safety reasons. Though this undertaking seemed fine in theory, since its intentions underpinned both the cub and scout philosophy of helping people, in practical terms the system often led to cruelty and abuse. Imagine a fresh faced, ten-year old cub dressed in full uniform, knocking on the door of a fifty-year old pederast and telling him, 'I'll do what you want for a shilling, mister!' It beggars belief.

Benny Benson would ask for his shilling in advance and then leg it. Old ladies were easy targets and kids would ignore their 'job done' sticker, placed on a door or window. My acolytes would then harass them for more dosh. Royston believed in the principle of 'share and share alike'. He would undertake tasks and have two books to be signed by employers indicating the nature of the job and the sum of money paid, rather like a crooked accountant. Royston always did well for penny chews, bottles of 'pop' and spangles during that week.

I issued my last 'job done' sticker in 1958. 'Bob A Job' week was usually early in March and my menu included car cleaning, painting fences, sweeping leaves and even shoe shining. Now, these types of chores weren't too bad, but I have never forgotten my final job. I knocked on the door of Mr Halliday in Lissadel Street, and was itching to get my card signed and then get off to the next house. Mr Halliday was a man who always dressed in a moth eaten grubby vest, shabby trousers with braces and a scruffy pair of slippers. I was asked to clean his back yard. The unshaven gentleman had no teeth, but had a roll-up permanently stuck to the middle of his top lip.

'Only, it's a bit of a state, mind,' he advised me in gum speak.

I went round the back gate and was confronted with mountains of junk and rubbish as tall as the pyramids. My cub loyalty and pride made me have a go. It took me all day and several intravenous glucose drips to get done. Not even a glass of Vimto from the old miser. At the end of my labours, I barely had enough energy to knock on the back door. Mr Halliday emerged from his lair and refused to give me my shilling unless I swept up. I'd had enough. Dyb, dyb, dyb? I put to one side my naïve egalitarian values and told him, in no uncertain terms, him where he could stick his broom. Job done!

Whit walks:
a girl's tale

'NOW STAND STILL OR I'LL never get this done. A bit of cooperation if you please, young lady?' My mother's brusque instructions related to yet another tedious dress fitting and were frequently punctuated with a slap on the legs as I unwillingly stood on the chair.

I hated this. It was yet another year preparing for my compulsory participation in walking with the scholars on Whit Friday. The preparation for this loathsome event had started about two months earlier. Pieces of lace, taffeta and satin, together with fabric remnants, suddenly appeared in the parlour and were then sewn together to make me and my little sister our dresses for this annual event. I wouldn't mind but my mother had the sewing skills of a blind surgeon. She once mended our George's trouser pockets for him only to find he could fit three fingers into one while his whole arm disappeared into the other. However, she meant well, so my dad would say.

Whit week, now referred to as a period of time around the May Bank Holiday, was an important point on the calendar for church and Sunday school participating families. It was a time for people to show their commitment to the faith and allegiance to their church. The programme for this ritual involved Protestants ceremoniously walking the streets of northern towns on the Monday, and we Catholics doing the same thing on the Friday. Our street contained an eclectic mix of faiths. Twelve Protestant families, known as 'Prodydogs', and ten Catholic families, referred to as 'Catlicks' or 'Left Footers' by the opposition. The Schuckmans were the only Jewish family in residence in the street and the rest were pagan, agnostic or orthodox apathetic.

My mum, assisted by my forceful Auntie Ada, were both active members of 'The Shilling a Week Club'. Such fiscal investment would ensure that I would have a shiny pair of patent leather shoes for the procession. My old shoes would be passed down to my younger sister, Marion. They were deemed good as new by Auntie Ada, having only been worn a few times since their purchase the year before. You didn't argue with Auntie Ada. She resembled a female version of W. C. Fields, having a large and bulbous red nose, moulded into this form by her predilection for milk stout and port and lemon chasers. Her pugnacious persona was as grand as her proboscis, forcing people to admit they would sooner leap from the Hoover Dam than to argue with her.

The morning of Whit Friday saw me, Marion and my brother Gerard visit neighbours and relatives before we assembled at St James' church. The purpose of these parochial ventures was to show this selected few that our family firmly upheld tradition and we were good Catholics. Comments like, 'Ooh doesn't she look nice! All in white an' all', came from Mrs Scanlon, our immediate neighbour.

'Is her underwear new too, Doreen?' inquired cousin Rita as she lifted up my dress to check. 'Here love, put this in yer money box. Ya look smashin' chuck!' she continued. A sixpence or shilling would then be pushed into our hands as a reward for this humiliation. This was the principle reason for our social visits and the money raised would buy us kids sherbet dips and a bottle of Vimto. The rest would be seized by my mother and used to finance next year's Whitsuntide shenanigans.

My younger brother Gerard, at nine years of age, was short and a little on the portly side. He was forced to wear green short trousers and matching jacket. Completing this hideous tailoring was a matching bow tie, making him resemble a Sumo Leprechaun. 'Bonny' was the term used by many to describe him, though we all knew it was a kind-hearted euphemism for 'fat'. Poor Gerard never received any more than a sixpence and would complain to me afterwards that he deserved ten bob for wearing that clobber.

More embarrassment followed, with us all being asked to march up and down in the street accompanied by yet more praise and adulation from passers by. Should it be raining, you might hear the venomous Mrs Rene Vickers, a Methodist extraordinaire, issue such unhelpful sectarian wisdom as, 'God knows his own!' or 'The sun shines on the righteous!'

Mr Pardoe always made it his place to congratulate us. We were never sure about this gentleman, a loner who lived as a lodger in an end of terrace on Ellor Street. We always got half a crown off him but were subjected to some hair stroking and bottom patting antics, forcing my mother to say, 'Got to be off now Mr Pardoe, if ya don't mind and thanks for yer generosity.'

'Hands to yerself Mr Pardoe and gerroff her bum!' was a remark from Auntie Ada that immediately concluded his disturbing physiotherapy.

The rendezvous for us scholars was immediately outside St James' church. There was little traffic about in those days and we could gather on the road without fear of being run over. Mr Aspinall and Mr Crowther, both church-wardens, would act as marshals and get all of us in groups in a certain order. At the front were the banner men responsible for carrying the church banner that bore an embroidered image of the Virgin Mary and underneath the words 'St JAMES' PENDLETON'. I was told that the original pennant carried an icon of St James himself but that mice had got at it in the vestry one winter. Chewed holes in the fabric of the banner gave it a new and curious identity featuring a decapitated saint and the words JAM PENDLETO underneath. A quick decision was made by Father O'Driscoll on the morning of the walk to deploy the reserve.

Carrying the 'flag' as we called it was not an easy job. Streamers came from the top of the poles and the bottom of the flag. These colourful ribbons were the responsibility of 'important' male and female churchgoers. The chosen few held on to these attachments with reverence and decorum. Strong winds would sometimes move the banner men along like the rigging of the Cutty Sark. One year the normally mild mannered and grammar school-educated Mr Copley was caused to utter strange words and profanities as he journeyed down Broad Street at fifteen knots.

Immediately behind the church standard marched the clergy, all wearing their fine robes. Father O'Driscoll, flanked by his subordinates,

Fathers Molloy and Machin, was head honcho at St James'. He would give you terrible penances at confession that would keep you purging your sins for weeks. He had the bonhomie of Rasputin and the warmth of a Siberian winter. Rather unsurprisingly, he was as popular as enteritis on a long distance coach journey. Priests were the most important agents of worship in the church, and were always followed by the altar boys and girls, each wearing a white surplice and long black cassock. Ossie Baker was the exception on this day. He was on his way to church, only to be stopped by his granddad who, having forgotten his front door key, instructed Ossie to crawl down the coal hole at the front of the house, drop into the cellar, and then to go upstairs and open the front door. Ossie had completed this mission several times before for his forgetful grandparent, and subsequently slipped into the cellar with the skills of a pot holer. He emerged at the door, his white surplice now charcoal grey and his face and hands covered with coal dust, and he looked as though he was about to play Othello, never mind attend to God.

Laurence Bateman was the youngest of the altar boys and carried a gold cross on top of a long rosewood pole. After two hours of bearing this accessory, a lack of concentration and commitment came over him and he was seen poking a fellow choirboy in the bottom with this crucifix. His final irreverent behaviour was settled by a hefty clout around the ears from Father O'Driscoll as he attempted to lift Mrs Cunliffe's pillbox hat from her head with the same holy artefact.

Next in line were us girls with the youngest at the front and the nine and ten year olds to the rear. We were a set of clones, all dressed in white, some with lace bonnets others with white and silver tiaras. Each one of us carried either a tiny floral posy or bouquet. Some children held on to a large individual flower and after half an hour's struggling to keep this object upright they became flower weary. They were encouraged by their accompanying mums to cease dragging it over the cobbles with shouts of, 'Hold yer lily up, Bella!' or 'Remember Enid, that's God's flower so hold it up towards heaven, love.'

Some of the small boys and girls would hold separate placards proclaiming 'God is Love' but again after two hours in the heat, often the 'GOD' and 'LOVE' would fall, leaving the child in the middle declaring the enigmatic message 'IS' to the bemused crowd.

Musicians of the bands accompanying your church set the pace of the walk. St James' had a pipe band all smartly attired in green tartan kilts and tall black, furry busbies. They added vibrancy to the parade. The drum major, a fifty-five year old gentleman named Eugene Goldberg who was of questionable Hibernian Catholic ancestry, flamboyantly tossed his baton high into the air only to drop it on several occasions and blame the sun for his lack of dexterity. The crowd of onlookers loved him. He would gyrate and dance around at the front of the band with the energy of a Derry Orange apprentice boy. The band would play numbers like 'The Leaving of Liverpool' and 'The Happy Wanderer', all fuelling his ostentatious movements. I remember snare drums being bashed with skins as tight as a Scouser's alibi. Des Morrisey, a huge red-cheeked block of a man, and a walking advert for hypertension and Type 2 diabetes, carried the big bass drum. He would set the rhythm and thump this object with unquestionable energy whilst perspiring profusely. Who said that men couldn't multitask?

Some churches had their own brass bands all kitted out in scarlet jackets and with caps with gold braid. Saxophones played next to cornets and trombones. The older band members played tuneful numbers like 'Sons of the Sea' and 'Colonel Bogey' with a harmonious air. Unexpected sounds, akin to flatulence, emanated from the less competent adolescent members of this brass section.

On very warm days, the pitch holding areas of the road surface together would melt and stick to your shoes. To remove such debris would involve hopping along on one leg whilst simultaneously ripping the black tar from the sides of your footwear. Your hands would be black with this stuff and woe-betide if you got it on your clean white shirt.

The walk from Broad Street to Chapel Street was always packed with onlookers either standing along the pavement or leaning out of windows in the shops and offices alongside. Cries of, 'Pick yer feet up, our Tony!' or 'Oy, Noreen, give us a smile, love!' cut through the morning air. Some of the young boys in the procession who were clearly embarrassed about being on show in their Sunday best would shout back, 'Stop gawpin' at me, Mam, will yo'!'

The men of the parish were usually last in line, grouping behind the boy scouts, sea scouts, cubs, brownies and girl guides. There would be a constantly changing membership of these senior walkers.

A particular pub on Chapel Street would act as a holding station for some male casualties offering pints of Chester's Mild as sustenance and medication. These same people would rejoin the procession later using a system of short cuts.

The cluster of middle-aged males would occasionally contain a Teddy Boy, conspicuous by his long jacket, drainpipe trousers and bright crepe-soled shoes. His hair was styled in a bunch of grapes at the front with the mandatory creamed DA at the rear. Many people were frightened of Teds with rumours of their use of cutthroat razors and knuckle-dusters. Terry Percival, the St James' Ted in our group, knew why he was there. He was on show for the girls who would line the parade and he would often be seen canoodling with some of his teenage admirers as the march stopped to let people cross the road.

It was an extremely long and tiring morning for everyone. The parade would finish about lunchtime in Albert Square. Thousands of marchers and their families would congregate there and I would have my orders to grab hold of Gerard and Marion and get them an ice cream. My mother would have caught the bus to Victoria station and then meet us outside the Colonial and Mutual Life Insurance building just off the square. Everyone had their own rendezvous. There was never anywhere for us to sit to rest our aching legs. Before we could recharge our batteries for the return march, the cry would ring out from the megaphone, 'St James' please!' and we were off again. This time we would walk back to Chapel Street along Deansgate.

The return journey was always at a slow pace as everyone showed signs of fatigue and the procession was noticeably shorter. Even the bands appeared to have less puff. The half way mark was easily recognisable for you could always smell the noxious vapour of hair-setting lotion coming from Rita's Hair Salon on Chapel Street. Many of the little ones didn't cope with this return leg. Marion started to cry and moan so my mother took her home. Gerard thought he would try a similar strategy but just got shouted at by my dad who had spent most of the morning in the Blackfriars public house, near Greengate and Irwell. It was deemed that Gerard would walk back to Pendleton or receive an almighty clout for lack of cooperation. Gerard duly obliged.

At the end of the day the young boys would change and put on their playing out clothes. Most of us girls would keep on our dresses and play less physical and untidy games than our brothers. I remember both merriment and happiness in the evening that followed. Adults in our street would chat and laugh, often their conversations fuelled by Mackeson's or Wilson's Pale Ale. Sandwiches and toffees seemed to be in endless supply as we journeyed from one house to another. Even the Schuckmans laid on a Kosher experience of chicken livers and gefilte fish which we all said was lovely. Gerard liked it so much he said to my mum 'Can't we become Jewish and eat this stuff, and we won't have to walk with the scholars?'

'Shut up, Gerard!' came the quick reply from mum, which really meant 'No we can't!'

The extended day was abruptly brought to a close when mums called us in from the street. Father O'Driscoll was back at the presbytery and sat in his favourite horse's hair armchair, musing on today's events. He always championed the use of holy water for aching feet and sore muscles. That evening, however, saw a different application of the fluid. The special holy water he poured in those twilight hours came from a large bottle that didn't say anything about water. Three or four glasses of the liquid induced a feeling of wellbeing and anaesthesia. Its label read JAMESON.

Remember, remember the 5th of November

I T SHOULDN'T HAVE HAPPENED, but it did. I had only meant to dry the mixture. I'm sure I had the correct ratio of ingredients. What on earth had gone wrong?

'In Town Tonight' was in full swing on the wireless, when an explosion worthy of El Alamein suddenly interrupted John Ellison's dulcet tones. The blast came from our kitchen, causing my dad's Senior Service cigarette to part company with his lips and land on his grey flannels. His trembling face and body, now ashen with shock, told me my experimentation with gunpowder could well have secured his early retirement from this world.

I had, in fact, blown the oven door off its hinges in my attempt to dry the mixture of charcoal, potassium nitrate and sulphur. An older boy whom I had met whilst on holiday at a Prestatyn caravan park had told me to use these chemicals to manufacture my own fireworks, emphasising that the ingredients must be dry. What better place to dry them than in our oven?

I soon became aware of not causing the sudden death of my parent because of the whacks he delivered to my legs, now glowing as bright as the rouge on a pantomime dame. Curse short trousers! That year I remember not being allowed out on Bonfire Night. Instead I was enlisted to help redecorate the kitchen, now draped in garlands of soot and possessing an oven minus its door.

Preparations for Bonfire Night, or 'Bonny Night', usually began towards the end of September. This celebration was a street-by-street event and there was a palpable rivalry between them. The principal aim was to build the biggest bonfire. Today's RoSPA (Royal Society for the Prevention of Accidents) directorate would suffer apoplexy, but health and safety considerations were a low priority in the fifties. Bonfires were built in streets and assembled close to houses. The Firework Code printed on the sides of boxes of Standard, Astra, Payne's and Lion fireworks was somewhat anaemic with its advice. The most instructive guidance was 'Light the Blue Touch-Paper and Retire'. These words proved to be a tragic irony for Mr Newgent, a capstan lathe operator from Weaste, who lit an air bomb with a shorter than average fuse. Mr Newgent did retire, but unfortunately twenty years earlier than he'd expected, and now with three incomplete digits.

Collections of anything combustible, ranging from old sofas to planks of wood, were grouped together to give a tall cone-shaped structure. Extra wood was piled near the fire and would be added through the course of the evening. One enterprising group of youngsters from Beard Street, Pendleton, was skilled at removing people's back yard doors at night. They would patrol the ginnels and back alleys of houses in neighbouring areas, not daring to rob from their own of course. Indeed, thieving from other people's stocks of wood went on all of the time, making it essential that guards were posted to protect their timber.

Most children would be given a small box of fireworks by their parents. To purchase more of the incendiaries we would beg outside pubs, shops and cinemas. These places drew lots of people, and hopefully lots of pennies would result. Our ruse was 'Penny for the Guy, mister?' The gang of reprobates to which I belonged had poor sculptural skills. Our Guy looked hideously misshapen. Its head was an old football bladder mounted on a settee cushion covered with a shirt. The guy had no neck and its head often rolled off on cold windy nights. A face drawn on a paper bag would be held around the bladder by a couple of pieces of my gran's knicker elastic. Worst of all were its legs. Raymond Crosby supplied his dad's trousers, into which he stuffed newspaper and cardboard. Raymond filled the left leg, which looked great, but ran out of packing material for the right one. An odd pair of hobnailed boots supplied the feet, tied to the legs with string. We thus boasted a mannequin that looked as though it was suffering from gout in its right foot and elephantiasis in the other. Guys were usually transported about in old prams, wheelbarrows or pushchairs.

I recall one year we had left preparations for Bonfire Night rather late. Jimmy Fairclough, a diminutive and sickly looking six year old who always had a streaming nose even in the Summer months, deputised as our Guy. We had to admit he really looked the part. Things were going well until his cover was nearly blown as he set free a loud shaft of wind as we were saying thank you for receiving a thrupenny bit from a lady from the corner shop.

Money generated from our 'Penny for the Guy' scrounging would be divvied up and then we would rush to the local newsagent to buy more fireworks. There was a fascination with these newly purchased explosives and, like other boys, I kept mine in my wardrobe. I couldn't resist looking at them and getting them out of their boxes and paper bags. All of this pre-match messing around frequently caused them to leak their contents and consequently the box would contain a tempting powder containing saltpetre, magnesium and iron filings.

It always seemed to be cold and foggy on Bonfire Night. We prayed for weeks that it wouldn't rain. Such grim weather forced your mother to turn you out on the street with a thick pullover, Wellingtons, and an old gabardine raincoat knotted at the front. Some form of headwear was also on her list. Mine was my old cub cap that just about fitted my head. I had to be careful not to lose it especially whilst bending over to light my fireworks.

Our huge bonfire was stacked on a cinder croft off Strawberry Road. This was the site of an old warehouse and suffered an air raid on Salford docks some years before. It was a tremendous space and one year we had an enormous pile of wood the size of a Ben Nevis. There were stacks of 'bunny wood', as we called it, at the side ready to top up the impending furnace. Planks of wood were manhandled and many of us fell victim to cuts on our hands and legs from rusty nails sticking out of the timber. Stained old mattresses, floorboards, tea chests and vegetable crates all burned well. I remember Mrs Austin giving her two fifteen year-old twins a pasting for chucking her old ottoman onto the fire with clean sheets and pillowcases still in it. The rule was a simple one; anything lying around looking old, dishevelled and combustible went on the fire. However, we thoughtfully drew the line at 'Old Vinny', a tramp whose manor was Chimney Pot Park.

Newspaper soaked in paraffin was often used to start the fire, particularly when it drizzled with rain. Pyromaniacs in some streets used petrol and were seen to lose their forelocks and eyebrows as the blaze was instant. Stuck on top of the huge pyre was our Guy, headless of course. We never did find a way of keeping the bladder on the trunk. Huge cheers from both adults and children filled the roasted air as the flames singed its trouser legs. Colours of yellow, red and gold quickly enveloped its form and completed the cremation.

Women would bring Parkin, toffee apples and old potatoes for baking in the embers. Treacle toffee, which had been baked in an enamel tray, was cracked open with a hammer. Children would chew this stuff only to find it would stick to their teeth and gums causing jaws to cement together. Little kids lost their milk teeth, NHS dentures would crack, gums would tear with this solidified molasses, and all in the name of enjoying yourself. Some idiot lobbed an unopened tin of baked beans onto the fire once, only to shower us with its molten contents when it exploded with the force of Krakatoa.

The fireworks started long before the bonfire was lit – usually two weeks before. The older boys thought chrysanthemum fountains and snowstorms were for wimps. The arsenal of these impatient youths contained only penny bangers, penny canons, air bombs, jumping jacks, aeroplanes and rockets. Irresponsible and downright dangerous experimentation with these goods was practised with alarming frequency. Jumping Jacks, or rip-raps as we preferred to call them, would soon disperse a crowd when lobbed at their feet by some half wit. Penny bangers thrown behind old people acted as an immediate laxative or prompted a visit to the coronary care unit.

There was one posse of kids from Lissadel Street whose behaviour was universally considered to be beyond the pale, even by Barry Donaghue, our local village idiot. These kids, I believe, would have occupied the shallow end of any gene pool. Life-threatening antics such as holding a Roman Candle and directing fire balls at people were certainly on their list. Rockets would be aimed at shop windows and stream across Frederick Road like Exocet missiles. Bangers would be posted through letter-boxes. All Barry and us younger boys had in our repertoire was chucking bangers down grids or into buckets of water. Tying two rockets

together was a favourite ploy for Barry in his attempt to achieve the first lunar landing. He hoped that one would ignite the other as two separate stages of the missile. What actually happened was that the milk bottle containing the rockets fell over towards him and I believe that evening Barry would have outpaced the USA's sprinter, Bobby Joe Morrow, as he was chased by this accelerating fireball.

Once the wood was burning away, crowds of people would gather, their faces illuminated by the flames, and their silhouettes cast against walls. Bystanders would change colour as their fireworks burned. Copper salts turned people green and potassium changed them to lilac. Ooohs and aaarhs poured from their mouths as silver fountains spewed burning magnesium and rockets exploded, emitting trails of gold and crimson. Mums and dads lit sparklers for their children. Some lit one sparkler from another. For me, that was the best way to do it because you needed a concentrated heat source to coax the encrusted iron filings to burn. Parents provided encouragement, shouting, 'Go on love, write yer name in th' air with yer sparkler!' This proved to be an unsurprisingly difficult task for eight-year old Lawrence McCann who couldn't even do it with a pencil and paper.

Catherine wheels were always a problem. It was getting them to spin. Residents didn't take kindly to you setting fire to them on their back door, the scorch marks just didn't come off. I recall Barry getting a hefty crack from one poor soul whose rear portal bore five charred rings and resembled the logo of the Olympic Games. Mrs Stefanowicz came to our rescue and allowed us to nail them to her washing line post. I found Catherine Wheels infuriating as they would often jam mid ignition and you would burn your fingers trying to bump-start their revolutions.

Smoke was everywhere and hurt your eyes but we all persevered. Barry was a bit of a crackpot, predictably my gran described him as 'not being wired up properly'. One night he threw an old tyre on the burning mass, causing a thick, acrid miasma to envelope all that stood around the fire. Not only was there coughing and spluttering from the already bronchitic crowd but we all finished the evening resembling the cast of the George Mitchell Minstrels.

One year the fire brigade was called to Rossall Street whose bonfire appeared out of control. The group of fire officers was beaten away with a yard brush brandished by an irate and menacing Mrs Irene Lindop. This lady was a tall and extremely largely proportioned woman who clearly called a yard brush a yard brush as she poked the fire rescuers into Hankinson Street. You would hardly describe the frequently inebriated Mrs Lindop as a *femme fatale*, though she got very close to belonging to this category one evening. She was run over by a fruit and vegetable wagon outside the Royal Oak pub and sadly the vehicle was irreparably damaged.

The morning of 6 November saw us all out of bed early. It was a day of anticlimax and sadness. We would have to endure another twelve months before we could relive that same excitement. The air was often still, and had the unmistakable smell of gunpowder and metal oxides. The fire still glowed and blackened bed springs projected defiantly from the smouldering mass.

An early morning ritual was to search for 'duds'. These were fireworks of any type that had refused to ignite. We would throw them onto the cinders and wait for them to explode, or carefully open them and collect the mysterious chemical mix inside. Some youngsters foraged for discharged fireworks and the biggest thrill was to collect rockets with their sticks still intact. Pets would eagerly journey outside having been quarantined the night before, trying to make sense of their territory.

We would now have to wait for another year to recite the poem taught us in our school,

> *Remember, remember the fifth of November*
> *Gunpowder, treason and plot,*
> *I see no reason why gunpowder and treason*
> *Should ever be forgot...*

Roll on Christmas!

The wind in the Willows

A S A CALLOW NINE-YEAR OLD, even I could understand why football pundits referred to Duncan Edwards as the most complete player. He was like a rock in defence and his intelligent play allowed him to menace the opposition and shoot with even greater power than fellow team-mate, Bobby Charlton.

My visits to Old Trafford in the fifties were made possible by my uncle John, a former Japanese prisoner of war, who was a United fanatic. I was also blessed with another of my late dad's brothers who followed rugby league. He too called himself a red devil but his allegiance was to Salford Rugby League Club and not to the Manchester United fraternity down by the docks.

The Willows, Salford's ground, was situated in a fairly respectable area of the city, close to Buile Hill Park, a neatly manicured landscape boasting flower borders, exhibition greenhouses and a large Victorian building formerly housing the Lancashire Mining Museum. The southern borders of the ground embraced the working class areas of Liverpool Street, Weaste and Seedley.

The 1955 to 1962 seasons at this ground saw the club floundering in mid to bottom table obscurity. In contrast, Swinton, Salford's immediate rugby-playing neighbours, playing at Station Road, were achieving greater success. 'The Lions' as they were called believed not only that their ground was superior to The Willows, for they had the tallest goalposts of all the league grounds, but also their team had the best quality players. The likes of Albert Blan, Ken Gowers, Johnny

Stopford were at the top of their game. The Duncan Edwards parallel in Lancashire rugby league at that time was the agile and talented Alan Buckley, another member of the Swinton squad.

I would share the attention of my uncles by going to Old Trafford one week and The Willows the next. I wore a red and white bobble hat that had plastic red stars on it with the photographs and names of the United stars on its rim. On days we went to see Salford, the woollen rim would roll up concealing my other loyalty. I longed for a red and white scarf but my mum's wages at the Pendleton UCP tripe shop could never stretch to one. I did, however, have a wooden rattle. It was a Second World War gas rattle that would render deaf anyone who was nearby. It even gave me tinnitus and my gran banned me from using it in the house when I broke the ceiling light. (I had been getting carried away whilst listening to the football results on our Bush wireless.)I had painted the rattle's frame red but unfortunately we didn't possess any white so the bare brown wood would suffice. On one side of the rattle I had etched the names of United's team and on the other I proudly inscribed in biro the names of the Salford squad, again rendering it fit for purpose at both venues.

It was a Saturday in mid January and raining heavily. It was cold rain, the kind of rain that spat at the pavement and would hurt your face as the wind mercilessly threw it against you. Somehow, that didn't seem to matter. We teamed up with several other devoted fans as we pushed our way against this wall of rain along Weaste Lane to the ground. Young lads splashed in the puddles whilst obediently following their dads like mischievous ducklings. My bobble hat was now full of water and its new found weight stretched the fibres down across my red face, making me look as ridiculous as a pantomime dame. Again, it didn't matter. We were too busy discussing the last home game and sharing a cautious optimism for today's performance.

We turned into the approach to the ground and bought a programme from an equally drenched young man with his cap firmly pulled down against the rain that peppered his body. The programme cost three pence and its front cover always showed a drawing of a Salford player being tackled by an opponent wearing a black and white hooped shirt. Inside were match reports from the last game, the league positions, the team sheet and adverts for Holland's pies and Fieldsends coaches. In this particular issue we were warned that next season the programme purchase price would increase to four pence, news that was met with indignation from supporters who were currently exposed to, at best, poor or mediocre team performances.

At the turnstiles the amorphous crowd squeezed its way through these narrow portals like a piece of cheddar through a grater. My uncle paid my one shilling and sixpence entrance fee. As we pushed against the inertia of this stubborn contraption it clanked and rattled in the way all turnstiles do, sounding like the winch mechanism on the Big Dipper at Blackpool's Pleasure Beach. The old man operating this machine joked with my uncle, his chubby red face complete with its varicose lines reflecting many years of commitment to the club and to Wilson's bitter. His laughter was suddenly interrupted by a bout of coughing which put paid to any further conversation.

Parts of the stand to our left looked tired and paint from its woodwork flaked and tumbled to the cinder-strewn terraces below like dandruff onto a shabby black suit. There was always plenty of room on these terraces and on dry days a black mist would rise from this clinker and dull your shoes as you stamped your feet to keep warm. Metal crowd barriers gnawed by the passage of time gave sanctuary and squatters' rights to old men who'd stood there for years and knew everything about the game.

I joined a couple of the lads I knew at the whitewashed wall adjacent to the pitch. You got a really good view there. It was a great place to be, just a few yards from play, and to witness gruesome close ups of players with blood trickling from their noses or hear some choice northern language as things didn't go a player's way. You could hear a manikin referee sternly reprimanding a six-foot-four loose forward for foul play and watch as the accused professed his innocence. The giant block of a man, head down in shame, would absorb his admonishment and turn to join his team mates sulking like a naughty schoolboy.

The crowd smelled of a curious mixture of ale and sharp tobacco smoke. The men looked cloned, all wearing long overcoats and cloth caps. Some supporters came by motorcycle and stood in the crowd flagrantly announcing their mode of transport, still wearing their crash helmet complete with goggles on top. In the main stand was a small enclosure for club officials and the 'bourgeoisie'. Here the club directors sat wearing their camel overcoats and trilbies. The club chairman puffed on a large Havana cigar, a sign of wealth and importance to the proletariat below. Alongside these dignitaries were their wives in fur coats, with painted faces, bouffant hair and Chanel Number Five. Expensive jewellery was further testimony of their fiscal status.

Looking at the stand opposite, the dull grey landscape of spectators would at points glow briefly, as Bryant and May matches lit pipes and Woodbines. Behind the stand lay a tapestry of chimney pots projecting from never ending lines of terraced houses. Our opponents on this day were Hunslet, and in contrast their ground was to be found in a south-west suburb of Leeds. Parkside, as it was called, was set in a frame of grey and black slag heaps, ash and scrub. At other grounds coal pits dominated the landscape, their lofty colliery winch wheels boldly rising against a shadowy sky.

The older male supporters were often joined by partisan women whose no nonsense match analysis made it unwise to upset them. Loud cries of 'Gerra bloody pair o' glasses, ref!' and 'Do that again ya big bugger and I'll come on t' pitch meself an' sort yer out,' were regular well-intended proclamations from these loyal Salford Amazons. Many of them had their hair in rollers protected by a scarf neatly knotted under the chin. Preparation for their Saturday night out in the lounge of The Langworthy Hotel had begun earlier in the day.

A rather tinny sounding public address system crackled its way through the damp air, announcing the teams for the afternoon. The broadcaster welcomed the opposition, Hunslet RLFC, pointing out that they would be playing in their team colours of myrtle, white and flame.

'What the 'ell's myrtle!' cried a young Salford devotee, who at the same time was displaying mucous candles from both his nostrils.

'It's a poncey green!' replied his dad from ten rows back. 'An' flame an' all is posh for gold. Ridiculous, they ought to talk proper. Still, that's Yorkshire for yer,' he concluded.

I looked towards the scoreboard and noticed there seemed to be more numbers piled up awaiting use on the visitor's side. This was pessimism in its extreme. Surely we were going to win this afternoon?

Kick off time this day was at 2.30pm. The logic of this was to maintain enough daylight for the crowd to see the game. Floodlights were expensive things to run, particularly on gloomy winter days, and Salford did not acquire them until 1965. Harold Macmillan would then tell us 'You've never had it so good!' but still money for new players was in short supply. I always wished the prime minister had announced this advice stood on a soap-box in Hanky Park, an extremely impoverished area of Salford. He would surely have returned to Downing Street a wiser man, complete with a northern recommendation about where he could stick his misguided, Old Etonian philosophy.

A small battalion of Hunslet faithful cheered with excitement as their team took to the field in Omo-white shorts, and green, white and gold shirts. Leather studs clacked against the concrete floor of the tunnel as they poured out onto the emerald-green blanket of a pitch. This verdant area had been patched with spades full of sand to help improve drainage and repair turf from last week's skirmish. Rain was still coming down hard and seemed to defy gravity as the unrelenting wind blew it horizontally across the stadium. Players ran across the pitch to keep warm and not just to freshen the blood supply to their sleepy muscles.

A slightly disappointing roar, not dissimilar to the sound produced by a pride of lions with laryngitis, slowly spread across the terraces as my team emerged from the home changing rooms beneath the popular stand. Heralding their appearance was an instant smell of wintergreen and liniment, duly diluted by the incessant rain. Clad in red shirts, white shorts and red and white hooped socks, the Salford players tore into the arena, apart from Albert Halsall, a mountain of a forward who always seemed allergic to pace. Albert applied the principle of the conservation of energy this afternoon and ambled onto the field of play.

There was a noticeable lack of shoulder pads in those days. Shirts had reinforced collars that still ripped in combat, and gum shields were the sole property of the world of boxing. An absence of shin pads, except for the hooker, was testimony to the steely courage of these players. Vaseline, smeared around the ears of prop and second row forwards, was to reduce friction as heads and shirts tore against each other in scrummages. Many of these gladiators with deformed noses and lack of front teeth had faces that were soon to look as engorged and angry as a troublesome haemorrhoid as they played this brutal sport. Their recompense for this physical pounding was 'boot money', and these low wages forced players to travel by public transport to the ground.

The match officials on this day jogged on the spot, in an effort to keep warm wearing their black and white socks, black shorts and shirt.

One man said they looked like the three stooges. Brylcreem seemed to be de rigueur for referees and linesmen in those days, their hair pasted back with the stuff, giving an encrusted sheen to their receding pates. White, anaemic legs resembling hairy celery, sporting knees as knobbly as a sack of coconuts were other anatomical essentials for the job. Referee Eric Clay was an exception; his corpulent excess coupled with his robust discipline made him as popular as Joe Stalin. Eric was hardly the most mobile of match officials but he always had a knack of being in the right place at the right time.

In terms of crowd control, the Saturday afternoon epic was usually self-policing. Over zealous disciples who became carried away with opinion and felt the need to enforce this view with their fists, were soon told by more senior onlookers who had recently suffered Hitler's wrath to 'pack it in and not to be so bloody stupid!' After all, the few police officers that were in the ground watched the game and not the crowd.

The match started and soon became the predictable brutish physical onslaught. Forwards drove against their counterparts picking up balls from the dummy half and lunged, heads down, at a wall of hard muscle. Drives like these tired defenders and with no four- or six-tackle rule to arrest this slow pace, the battle fatigued players gasped for air amid laboured rucks. Shoulders were dropped and used as battering rams against a human barricade which held as firm as the Hoover Dam. Crunching tackles, with often three bodies thumping against one, saw sweat and spit whiplash into the air on impact.

The tedium of beef against brawn was often interrupted by sudden bursts of pep and vigour. A scrum half weaved left and right as elusive as a slippery eel. His sharp twists and turns left players determined to spoil his pace and agility. Arms stretched out in vain like men trying to flag down an errant taxi. His cunning and nimble moves had changed the tempo of the game and secured cheers from the crowd. The enjoyment was abruptly halted as this whippet-like soul was caught by a man twice his size. His body was slowly enveloped in a tangle of arms and legs like an octopus engulfing its prey.

By half time it seemed impossible to tell each team apart, and even the fullbacks were daubed in generous helpings of Salford loam. Scrums had lacerated the pitch and rain turned turf into mud. The quagmire from this battle of a sport made the fields of Passchendaele seem like firm ground.

A cup of hot Bovril at the end of the first period brought warmth back again to my fingers. It was scalding hot and always scorched my throat as I swallowed it. On many occasions club officials took an open blanket along the touchline and loyal supporters would toss some loose change into it. The loudspeaker would make an announcement about some player whose career had been cut short by injury and would benefit from the collection.

The second half brought more scrummages which frequently led to more kicked points than tries. The fading shafts of daylight now picked out shimmering lines of water vapour coming from the twelve men locked together in a jigsaw of sinew, fat and bulk. It reminded me of the spent steam emerging from the cooling towers of Agecroft power station. The composite mass of the scrum was a fusion of over two hundred stones in weight testing Newton's laws of motion.

Club newcomer Les Bettinson, a centre signed by the legendary Gus Risman, and who would go on to serve Salford for many years, weaved his way through the Hunslet line and put us ahead with his intelligent play. The advantage, however, was soon lost as the illustrious Brian Gabbitas broke through an exhausted Salford defence.

Bruises, contusions, sprains, haemorrhage and concussion were all treated with the same prescription. Triage was the club physio who would run onto the field in his woollen tracksuit, carrying a towel, bucket and magic sponge. A disregard for blood-borne diseases ensured that a player's cut above the eye was washed with the same wipe as another's gashed leg. A cranium soaked in cold water from the sponge revived many a player flattened by a subtle uppercut or stiff-arm tackle.

Injuries such as a broken leg or a coma called for the attendance of two members of the St John Ambulance. It was always embarrassing for them when one of the duo, eager to implement his life-saving training, slipped over in the mud as he dashed to the casualty. The crowd would respond to this mishap with bursts of laughter. I always thought the stretcher they carried should be bigger because whole sections of the injured soul's body dangled lifelessly over its edge. Their public humiliation grew to even greater heights if they dropped their supine patient.

The final whistle put paid to this merciless skirmish just as John Cheshire, another of Salford's talented centres kicked for touch. The ball burst the ozone layer and slowly descended back to planet earth, bouncing off the roof of the main stand and falling into the crowd below. By now the players were unidentifiable, soaked and plastered in dark brown mud. Exhausted gladiators who minutes before had participated in a contest of beef against brawn, and often fist against face, now shook hands and slowly drifted towards the tunnel. Congratulations were issued in a staccato language punctuated by gasps of air. This mud-encrusted homogenous troupe resembled a cast auditioning for 'The Al Jolson Story'. A hot bath and a long soak would soon restore their individuality though.

The Hunslet team boarded their coach for the trans Pennine journey home. Some of us juniors were let onto the charabanc for autographs and we meandered our way past crates of ale and a miasma of Park Drive. A front row forward sat nursing a black eye and cut lip. Gulping a bottle of Tetley, his body seemed to defy the rules of anatomy, as his head appeared fused to his shoulders with an absence of a discernable neck.

I still have the somewhat scrawled names in my old autograph book and such classics as Geoff Gunney, John Griffiths, Brian Gabbitas and Fred Ward stand out. Seeing them in collar and tie, their bodies now clad in sports jackets and long overcoats, gave them a more ordinary appearance.

Our final duty was to queue outside the players' entrance to see our team as they too exited the ground in overcoats and caps. Some carrying a duffle bag, some with a small leather suitcase, came through the door to then stand at a bus stop or to walk their way home.

'Will ya sign this for us Frank? Will ya sign this Roy?' came the eager requests from the junior faithful. Maybe a few pints tonight to help anaesthetise their bruises and sprains? Back to work on Monday. Some down Agecroft Pit, some in the engineering yards of Trafford Park, others as labourers for Salford Council and some white collar workers too. These were my unforgettable heroes of this tough northern game.

Some of my Salford team, 1958–1960

Fullback	Arthur Gregory
Wing	Albert Baines
Centres	John Cheshire, Les Bettinson
Stand Off	Jackie Brennan, Syd Lowdon
Scrum Half	Billy Banks, Harold Gregory, Terry Dunn
Prop	John Hancock Albert Halsall
Hooker	Frank Boardman
Second Row	Harry Council, Roy Stott
Loose Forward	Bryn Hartley, Hugh Duffy
Salford's first ever substitute	Terry Loughlin

Once upon a time...

'**I**'M NOT WEARING THAT, MAM! It makes me look deranged.'
    'It looks alright to me,' shouted my gran, who had just lit a Park Drive and was now sipping the top off a glass of Threlfall's bitter.

Her opinion did little for my self-confidence. After all, she'd knitted my cousin Bernard a balaclava last year and the hole for his mouth was in the wrong place. To this day he still contorts his lips when he speaks. My mum says he talks like a ventriloquist with a palsy.

'I don't care, mam. I can't wear this.' These were my final words, and reflected an abject despondency about her needlecraft.

The article of clothing to which I was referring was my mum's attempt at making me a Davy Crockett hat. My mate Herbie had a belter, bought from Barmy Mick on Salford market. Mind you, its fur tail did drop off after three weeks of Indian fighting and it was also quite noticeable that when he wore this head-piece, cats would pursue him. Mine was made from Auntie Cissie's fox fur stole. Its long, bushy tail didn't look too bad, it was the hat itself that was hideous. It was so big it made me look as though I was being mauled by a savage beast. There was even a bit of its foot sticking out the side.

I remember standing in a queue outside the Gaumont cinema on Deansgate in Manchester with my mum. Every kid wore a Davy Crockett hat – recognisable Davy Crockett millinery. I was the pathetic soul wearing what looked like road kill. Some kids had plastic muskets and one lad from Lower Broughton sported a laced brown jacket with tassels, the likes of which even Fess Parker himself would have envied. My mate David, whose mum and dad had a baker's and confectioner's in Eccles, made his cluster of juvenile frontiersmen, powder horns by wrapping brown paper around cream horn moulds. Our young Crockett wannabe was subsequently flogged by his father for a drop in shop profits.

It was lashing it down with rain, real Manchester rain, and the queue ran back as far as Kendal Milne. However, such atrocious weather did not spoil our determination to enjoy the film. There came from the crowd an adenoidal loyalty, supporting our hero. We sang:

> *Born on a mountain top in Tennessee,*
> *Greenest day in the land of the free,*
> *Raised in the woods so's he knew every tree,*
> *Killed him a bear when he was only three,*
> *Davy, Davy Crockett, king of the wild frontier.*

There was little alternative but for me to volunteer for the part as a Creek Indian. Rather than tax my mother's creative talents, I decided to make my own head dress using fly-paper and feathers obtained from Uncle Cyril's pigeon loft. The fly paper did hold the feathers in place but in the summer months it also acted as a cemetery for blue bottles.

Going to the cinema and watching the television in those days spawned a desire among us urchins to re-enact these epics. Bomb-sites doubled as forts and castles. Sheets propped up with a pole or draped over a washing line were tents. Dens were built from old planks, beer crates and clothes maidens. If you needed a horse you galloped along the road slapping your thighs whilst holding on to imaginary reins. Broad Street and Frederick Road were the Texas Plains. Girls often played the role of horses, their pig tails acting as reins. This was particularly useful when we were copying Ward Bond's wagon train under Indian attack. Tomahawks were fashioned from a large piece of flint held firmly in place by the jaws of a monkey wrench. Axes were constructed from a piece of split wood and a triangular piece of slate lashed into place with parcel string. Neolithic man had nothing on us.

Dustbin lids acted as shields, clothes props were jousting lances and two bits of wood nailed together passed as swords. Brooms were Red Indian spears and half bricks were grenades. By now, you will be able to imagine the sorts of accidents and injuries sustained from using such an arsenal. Pea guns caused many an ear to glow scarlet and throb to the beat of your heart. Swinging bits of wood to defend your country made bruising, splinters and cuts the *plat du jour*. Milbro aluminium catapults were responsible for emergency visits to Manchester Eye Hospital. Homemade catapults, constructed from rubber inner tubes, could hurl large stones for miles, making Roman ballistas look quite average. Sandy's younger brother suffered five sucker marks on his forehead when Sandy used a bow and arrow in an attempt to portray William Tell and knock an apple from his head.

William Tell gave everyone a problem in that no one had a crossbow. We used to turn our bows and arrows on their side to simulate such weaponry. My mum joked that Ernie Saunders, the Smiths Crisps representative, would have made a good William Tell, because he was always making overtures to her and Auntie Minnie. When we did have a go at playing William Tell, Tommy Corless, who nobody liked, insisted on playing Landburgher Gessler, mainly because he had a plastic sword with a red bead in its handle. Most of our plays ended up in a fight and kids whacked other kids' swords with their own. Battle scenes worthy of inclusion in the film Braveheart ensued. Less coordinated soldiers struck blows to knuckles and the conflict deteriorated into fisticuffs yielding black eyes and fat lips. I wanted our plays to be as factually correct as possible and I remember reprimanding Tommy Corless when he was about to torture William Tell (Jacky Beardall). Landburgher Gessler, I pointed out, would not have been smoking a woodbine at the time. Tommy seemed unimpressed, and his response was to give me a brief verbal reply that had something to do with the male anatomy. The television programme itself amused me. The star, Conrad Phillips, was once seen doing battle with Gessler's men on the shores of what was supposed to be Lake Lucerne. In one shot a Morris Oxford was seen motoring along the A4086 on the other side of the lake. Also, interior scenery was badly constructed and waved about, putting the production into the same appalling league as Crossroads in later years.

The thing that gave everyone excitement was to dress up. Pillow cases with head and arm holes cut out of them, acted as tabards worn by medieval knights. Mrs Scanlan was non too pleased with her son's portrayal of Ivanhoe. He'd donated five of these for him and his acolytes to look the part. She growled at her son, who was now in floods of tears after having received a pasting worthy of an assault by Joe Louis.

'What's going to go on the bed now? Bloody suits of armour, ya stupid kid?'

The advent of the string vest in the fifties was a blessing for us kids. It doubled as chainmail. Streets were full of paediatric knights of the realm running around in their dad's underwear. Girls made pointed hats out of cardboard and had the customary ladies scarf, hanging from its tip. Mum's dresses gave authenticity to their role in our medieval plays.

As kids, we were indebted to Corn Flakes boxes. You could make a good knight's helmet out of one of them. Symmetry and mathematics were beyond Walter Kipple. He never seemed to be able to draw in the correct positions for eye and mouth holes on the box. Playing at Knights of the Round Table proved difficult for both Walter and his asthma and he would frequently pause to remove the structure that was causing him asphyxia. We would momentarily suspend our skirmish and in amazement observe Walter's colour change from blue back to white. As soon as this end point had been reached we then felt licensed to stab him once more with impunity. You didn't have to be skilled in origami to fold copies of the *Football Pink*, *Daily Mirror* or *Empire News* into terrific head gear.

Kellogg's also provided us with free gifts such as plastic frogmen you would stuff with baking powder and watch go up and down in a milk bottle full of water. The rear of the box often contained drawings of objects you could cut out. One favourite was a pirate's hat and eye patch. In our street, my gran said she'd never seen so many partially sighted buccaneers who'd apparently overdosed on corn flakes in an attempt to get at the box. Another cut out was a boomerang. I cannot remember the year Kellogg's offered this but I am sure it will come back to me.

Morris Barlow had one of those plastic toy daggers with a spring blade that retracted when you stabbed someone. Morris showed his auntie how it worked but unfortunately the spring jammed on this occasion and his aunt was soon on her way to Salford Royal requiring four stitches. Maisie Trott's dad was a teacher and she could get bottles of red Quink ink that acted as blood for us to apply to imaginary wounds. Morris's auntie, however, shed the real thing.

Grans' corsets provided us with pink and white stays used for modelling, unbeknown to our grans. You could make anything from them, leaving your gran bulging in places where nature had been cruel. Indeed, a corset itself made a great breast plate for a budding Sir Galahad, although its standard pink colour gave you a look more of a queen than a knight.

Most of us, excluding the girls of course, wanted beards or moustaches to give our characters both maturity and authenticity. Cotton wool was the obvious material and was available in great supply. We would dye it in black ink to stop us all looking like Father Christmas. One kid from Florin Street had a really impressive handle bar moustache he'd made from paste and dog hair. As we played 'Bandits at Three O'clock' ridding the skies of Stukas and Messerschmitts, his dog, now with a look of alopecia, trundled along behind.

Mums unknowingly provided their daughters with cosmetics that would strengthen the credibility of the parts they played. There were red lips worthy of Jane Russell, more mascara than Elizabeth Taylor had ever seen, and rouge-plastered petite cheeks that would have given Jayne Mansfield a run for her money. I recall giving Giles a reprimand for using excessive amounts of the stuff in his role as Geronimo. Although red lipstick daubed in lines across his cheek made him look the part, I pointed out that such a revered Indian chief would not have had the lips of Kim Novak. I also thought the use of eau de Cologne made him less macho, and hardly a credible historical figure. Yes, even at the age of nine, many of us were concerned about Giles's demeanour.

It was usually boys who dominated the principal roles in our games. Girls had more subordinate parts and acted as nurses, farmhands, queens, duchesses and the general proletariat. Bertha Lythgoe, however, was the exception. Bertha would scrap with anyone. Boys would elect to chew glass than to challenge her. Bertha was the consummate demagogue and her rendition of Hitler was truly scary. Her speech to rally her Wehrmacht (actually an army of seven which also included Ronny Kirkwood's dog) contained enough vitriol and persuasion to make the parachute regiment scatter down Hankinson Street.

'I wouldn't want a clout from her!' reasoned General Montgomery (Eugene Mulcahay). Eugene was a sociopath who would frequently beat up his dad.

Perhaps her most formidable leadership role was when we decided to re enact scenes from the film 'The Vikings'. Bertha's ferocious nature would have put the wind up Odin himself. The trouble was that because of Bertha's reputation, everyone wanted to be on her side and we were desperately short of Anglo Saxons to pillage. Bertha suggested that we should be as credible Vikings as possible, and travel by longship. To achieve such realism we lashed some scaffold boards together and tied three tin baths on top of them for greater buoyancy. Constructing it like this also gave us somewhere dry to sit. The ship's broad mast was a sheet from George Dougan's bed. Later he would get a real leathering from his mum for losing this item. Because of ownership and also because we couldn't work out how to keep it upright, George was given the job of holding the long pole on which it was nailed.

Our North Sea, across which we would travel, was 'The Cut' canal off Frederick Road. To my amazement, the longship defied Archimedes and actually floated. It remained above the water surface until all of the Nordic warriors wanted to climb aboard. Bertha took charge of the embarkation and calculated that the vessel would only hold three Vikings, leaving the other seven to walk along the towpath waving their swords. It started off well but soon our female Kirk Douglas, who was humming the film's theme tune, noticed her sailors were reducing in number as the craft journeyed some fifteen yards in the direction of Manchester. Jumping into the canal was like throwing yourself into a soup of diphtheria and polio. You could catch anything from its waters, ranging from cholera to legionella. Minus a crew of two, Bertha boldly continued towards the edge of the flat world (Greengate and Irwell Rubber Works) whilst those who abandoned ship, and took in lungs full of water, became certain candidates for Valhalla (Hope Hospital). Our play was brought to an abrupt finish when someone on the towpath shouted, 'Copper!!' Our brave Norsemen, unfortunately not brave enough to stand their ground and support their female Einar, decided to leg it, leaving the Salford City policeman to sort her out. Well, actually, it was the other way round.

The noticeable lack of trees where we lived made it difficult to play Robin Hood. Sherwood Forest around our way was a manky privet bush that had remarkably withstood incendiary devices dropped by the Luftwaffe some years earlier. It grew on a bomb site behind The Bridge pub, a lonely and abused botanic specimen, surviving shrapnel and kids carving their initials into its puny stem.

To gain a more realistic screenplay we had to walk to Buile Hill Park. This terrain boasted bushes, sycamore trees and steps up to the museum that doubled as Nottingham Castle. The parky went berserk when we lit the statutory fire that featured in all of our productions. Sadly, the toilets near the museum had to be demolished by the council, soon after the blaze got out of control. I did point out to Cyril Laidlaw that his milk bottle full of petrol was unnecessary. At the time, Cyril was playing the role of Will Scarlett, ironically a surname that vividly described his face after pouring the stuff onto the smouldering mass of twigs.

Diane Mascal was an attractive girl with smooth alabaster skin and beautifully groomed flaxen hair with not a nit in sight. She had lips you just wanted to kiss and she was the obvious choice for Maid Marian. Diane wore her mum's costume jewellery, and its simulated diamonds complemented her eyes that sparkled like stardust and reflected a depth of universal love. By now you can tell I had a crush on Diane and I truly believed she would fall for the intellectual and enigmatic persona I was so desperately trying to create. Sadly it was not to be. I never featured on her calling card. She eventually married a scaffolder from Droylsden whose sideburns resembled a wall of ivy.

We were about half way through replaying the scene where Robin Hood first met Little John, and there was to be a dual using wooden staffs. My sturdy weapon was a broom we used to sweep the back yard, and I got a clout from my gran when it broke mid combat. We had to make do with any bits of wood, because you see, there were staff shortages, even in those days. The storyline of this first meeting was to acquaint Robin of Loxley with the courage and strength of Little John and subsequently he would be recruited into the Sherwood foresters. It was to take place in an entry between two rows of terraced houses. The drainage channel that ran between these two sets of properties acted as the stream, and a plank of wood across it doubled as the bridge on which the meeting should take place. I took the role of brave Robin quite seriously, so too did Bertha with her role (an ideal choice for the part of Little John), principally because of her dimensions and aggression. My mate Herbie would say of Bertha that one look from her and the desert would freeze. She had testosterone by the gallon.

The play was progressing really well. I'd already struck a pre-skirmish deal with Bertha to go easy on me. Should I be rendered brainless from one of her blows, the show could not go ahead for continuity reasons since I was writer/director. I was about to enlist Little John into my band of followers when this historically accurate scene was corrupted by Walter Kipple. This woeful urchin came from nowhere, swinging on a rope he had attached to a girder sticking out from the roof of the Hudson's outside toilet. His journey took him right into the middle of our scene. Walter was dressed only in a pair of ill-fitting, tatty white underpants that looked as though they had suffered years of abuse from carbolic, bleach and Dolly Blue. Walter's naked anatomy reflected the fact that you could see more meat on the nits in a tooth comb. His pale skin left us convinced he had only one red blood cell in his body. His skinny chest with protruding ribs, made him look like a park bench when he lay down.

His entrance was heralded by screaming noises, making everyone turn to see this pathetic, malnourished specimen catapult himself into the centre of our play.

'Wot the 'ell are you doin', Walter?' I screamed, 'You're spoiling the scene!'

'I'm Tarzan,' he replied in a pathetic whimper, as he landed clumsily on his bottom, just missing our fire.

'Tarzan?' questioned Charlie Sago, who was playing a terrific Friar Tuck. 'Tarzan? You look more like Ghandi! Now bugger off and find Jane, Walter. You're givin' us snow blindness.'

More contemporary conflicts demanded a change in weaponry and costume. Films such as 'Dunkirk', 'Reach For The Sky' and 'Camp on Blood Island' provided us with plenty of play. Scenes involving Japanese soldiers usually concluded by them committing hara-kiri and then getting up to fight again. Sandy Krink got a bit carried away with this ritual. He portrayed a courageous soldier, loyal to the Japanese flag, wearing his cub cap with a handkerchief hanging from the back. Sandy did, in fact, stab himself in the ribs with his gran's knitting needle when Frankie Beardall patted him on the back during the suicide simulation. Yet another trip to Salford Royal.

The film 'The Dam Busters' got us into a lot of trouble. Still with its theme tune ringing in our ears, we set about demolishing the Mohne Dam. Unfortunately for Ernie Devlin, publican of The Bridge public house, we chose his property to implement Operation Chastise. The pub had a six-foot wall around the side of the building and the use of the past tense 'had' could now be ascribed to its architecture. Budding Guy Gibsons would fly towards the wall with their Avro Lancaster arms outstretched. The lad tagging along in his wake was the bomb aimer complete with a couple of large bricks, which he would hurl against the wall. The raid took slightly longer than Squadron Leader Gibson's assault. In fact, it took two hours for the wall to crumble and was helped along half way through the bombing by Stefan Podgorsky's dad's lump hammer. I cannot accurately remember the number of direct hits that we received from Mr Devlin when he discovered the destruction caused by our Dam Busters Tribute Band. However, I do remember getting another dose from my gran after she had collected her nightly jug of ale from him that evening.

And so, once upon a time, whatever epic was selected, whatever drama and conflict took place and whatever the injuries and mortality sustained ... they all lived happily ever after.

Oh, I do like to be beside the seaside

'**A**RE WE THERE YET, MAM?'

My cry competed with the rush of steam and clanking sounds as the train pulled out of Salford station. There was I, an excited eight year old, about to embark on our annual holiday to Blackpool.

'Are we there yet? I've told you when we will be there Ronny. Look for the Tower, but not now. We've only just set off!' replied my mum, as she searched through a bag, and separated our fish paste sandwiches from the buckets and spades.

I continued to press my face against the compartment's cold window, at times wiping away the condensation from my breath. A further twenty minutes of horizon searching produced yet another eager inquiry.

'Is that the Tower, mam. That thing sticking up over there?' My grubby finger pointed to the distant horizon.

'That's one o' them electricity pylons, yer puddin'. Stop mitherin' me Ronny. It won't be for another hour yet. We're not even at Preston!' she shouted.

'And leave that leather strap alone too. We don't want the window down. It's cold enough in here already.'

The disappointment on my face soon eased with a self prescribed penny chew taken from the pocket of my short trousers. My vigil continued.

The flatness of the Fylde coast gives an early warning of your approach to Blackpool. Suddenly, the tip of the Tower appears as an unmistakable harbinger of a week's fun-packed holiday in the famous Lancashire seaside resort.

It always made me smile, even at an early age, that when you told someone you were going on your holidays next week they would reply, 'Are you going anywhere nice?' What a stupid question! Of course we were going somewhere nice. We certainly wouldn't have saved up all year to go to Scotty Road in Liverpool or Moss Side. Some families in our street always went to Rhyl, a resort on the North Wales coast and always rated far lower than Blackpool. I overheard our coalman saying that he thought people went to Rhyl if they believed Blackpool too la-di-da.

The train journey to Blackpool finished at either Talbot Road or Central Station. During the month of August in the fifties, trains would arrive from Lancashire towns and cities at the rate of one every three minutes. Kids would hurriedly wrestle with the brass door catch before jumping down onto crowded platforms. Immediately the bracing sea air, laden with a curious mixture of vinegar and vaporised candyfloss, would tell you that you had arrived at this holiday paradise and you were going to have a wonderful time.

Unless you had a few bob, you stayed in a boarding house in one of the roads at right angles to the sea front. If your experience at such a residence had been good the previous year, you booked there again. We stayed at Mrs Ivy Turner's Abide With Me Guest House on Albert Road, only a short walk from the station. Mrs Turner was a former captain in the Salvation Army and ran her boarding house like many Blackpool landladies did, with precision and a 'no nonsense' approach to the hospitality trade. We were half board and our day began by being woken by Mr Turner's percussion antics, thumping the huge gong in the hall. Residents became conditioned to this sound and performed like Pavlov's dogs, pouring into her front room for breakfast, which doubled as the dining area.

It was always tea in those days, no coffee. A glass of fruit juice gave you that extra special feeling of being on holiday. The butter in the butter dish was always curled and fluted and implied five star treatment. After your dose of cereal, eggs and bacon and use of the cruet, for which you were charged sixpence at the end of your stay, you were encouraged to leave the premises as quickly as possible. This decree also applied even if it was lashing it down with rain. In the evening, the front door was locked at ten thirty sharp. Asking her for a possible return at eleven fifteen was received like asking her to take a fiver off your bill.

'Rules is rules!' was her eloquent reply.

We never had a room with a sea view. Invariably it was a back yard vista festooned with washing lines and dustbins. We shared a bathroom and toilet facilities on the landing. Lying in bed and wanting to 'go', then hearing floorboards creak outside your door, meant someone had beaten you to it. You then had to linger in discomfort for a further ten minutes.

Middle class visitors would stay in hotels along the sea front. These establishments had sun lounges where residents could take afternoon tea served by pimply waiters in white jackets. Guests read copies of the *Daily Mail* and sheltered in the warm during inclement weather. The largest and most exclusive was The Imperial. My gran would say of its residents, 'They're so posh that lot, they get out of the bath to wee.'

A tram ride north of The Imperial took you to another large hotel, built with the architectural design of a medieval castle. It was The Norbreck Hydro. Again, we thought you must have a few bob to book in there. It was, however, considerably cheaper than The Imperial and in a different league. It just looked such an imposing and extraordinary building. You expected to bump into Sir Gawain and the Green Knight at reception.

The Golden Mile is a stretch of seafront from the Pleasure Beach to North Pier. Its atmosphere was both exciting and intoxicating. The noise was constant. Bells ringing, men shouting, laughter, tunes from an organ, noises from amusement machines all fused together to give a magical cacophony that drew you in. Here, there were prizes to be won, fortunes to be told, seafood to be devoured and rock of all shapes and sizes to take home.

Interspersed along this parade was the occasional pub of which The Manchester was the largest. My gran would consume her twice-daily dose of Mackeson's at this hostelry, or sometimes at The Gynn in Gynn Square on North Shore. A Yates's Wine Lodge, selling precious little wine and previously referred to as a spit and sawdust pub, nestled just off the front in Talbot Road. Serious drinkers frequented this place and when it was Glasgow holiday week, pints of Chester's mild supped at this place were followed by pints of A-Rhesus negative at the infirmary. Another pub off the seafront boasted 'Champagne On Draught'. Blackpool gave you everything.

The stalls and marquees along this busy and pulsating boulevard added to Blackpool's appeal. Gypsy Petulengro read heart and life lines as long as you crossed her palm with silver beforehand. Billed as a clairvoyant, Gypsy P from Accrington once upset my gran when she announced to her she was closing down for the day, to which my gran replied, 'If you're that good a clairvoyant, lady, then ya should have ruddy well known I was comin'!'

Next door was Pablo's Ice Cream Parlour serving all flavours of the most mouth-watering gelato. The Tattooed Lady showed her skin artistry alongside Mick's Shellfish Bar, where you could purchase marine wildlife from winkles to Fleetwood crabs. Gypsy Rose Lee charted your longevity and her crystal ball gave hope of marriage to peroxide blonde mill girls from Burnley. Joke shops sold fart cushions that would cheer up Christmas parties, and itching powder that made your auntie's skin red raw.

Chip shops always did a brisk trade. Fish and chips were fried in beef lard adding that irreplaceable and unique flavour. It would stimulate your taste buds and line your arteries at the same time. Portions were wrapped in newspapers, telling of news such as Sir Anthony Eden's attitude towards The Suez crisis. Our prime minister was blissfully unaware his words were keeping warm our steak puddings, gravy and mushy peas. Some kids would be seen trying to make that impossible first bite into a toffee apple whilst others walked along with candyfloss beards and moustaches.

Amusement arcades incorporated Bingo stands where callers bellowed cryptic information through cheap microphones.

'Doctor's orders – number nine!'

A cry of 'Legs eleven!' would be followed by old ladies wolf whistling through badly fitting NHS dentures. Optimistic cries of 'House!' were rewarded with a voucher for a set of saucepans. Unfortunately you needed five such tickets to win this kitchenware and your thirst for success forced you to play another game.

Slot machines at 'a penny a go' gave you potential to win a shilling. Machines where pennies displaced more pennies abided by the laws of gambling statistics and most of the time you went away disappointed and skint. Cranes with grabs seldom rewarded you with a soft toy bear as you furiously wound its wheel. The toy frequently dropped off just before the delivery chute. Boys played on 'Tail End Charlie' simulators hoping to do their bit against the Luftwaffe. Some inquisitive lads were suddenly pulled away from 'What The Butler Saw' machines by an embarrassed parent. Ball bearings were spun round spiral tracks in Allwin slot machines and if the ball dropped into the right hole you'd win a small pack of spangles. Youngsters were drawn to other slot machines to watch with a morbid curiosity things such as 'Death by Guillotine'. Poorly made automaton models with faces painted as an afterthought twitched their way through this appalling re-enactment.

Parents prayed for fine weather. Cries of 'Dad, it's tippling down!' meant long periods of time in the arcades of the Golden Mile and holiday budgets were dashed. Visits to Olympia and the Tower also placated miserable, wet children but were equally damaging to finances. There was nothing cheaper than a day on the sands.

Throughout the summer, Blackpool beach remained packed with holidaymakers. Even at low tide there was barely room for the population of the North West who would descend from the prom, all determined to 'have a good time'. At two pence a day for a deckchair, dads carried these striped canvas seats to their square metre of beach paradise. It was a particularly hazardous journey on windy days. Sand would blow onto the promenade and get into your hair and ice cream.

Older people seemed reluctant to reveal any parts of their anatomy or even to dress in casual clothing. Men would sport knotted hankies to shield bald pates. Sixty-year old males sat in their deckchairs booted and suited and looking as though they were waiting for a job interview. Trousers rolled up to the knees for a paddle was as far as they would go. Such bare foot liberty would allow all kinds of flotsam to collect around their ankles as they padded through the shallows. Kids were warned of jellyfish yet some fearless youths would seek them out and poke them senseless with their spades. Ladies would daringly raise their skirts a few inches to catch a well-earned dose of ultra violet. Three pints of Wilson's bitter, quaffed at lunchtime by your dad, would induce in him an afternoon coma. His pathetic unconscious figure lay collapsed in a deckchair. After an hour of snoring and dribbling he would regain contact with the living world once more. His face was fiery red and sore. I remember my mum saying to him, 'Ya look as though you've been apple bobbing in a chip pan, George! That'll hurt tonight.'

I can picture my gran lounging in her deck chair, complete with overcoat and 'Kiss Me Quick' hat, quietly taking the afternoon air. On one occasion, from nowhere a plastic football shot through the air and struck her on the head. Her usually ashen complexion now contrasted with a reddened and swollen ear. Trauma of such magnitude forced her to snap and to reprimand her uncoordinated young assailant.

'Of all the ruddy heads on this beach you have to hit mine. Now bugger off away from me or I'll call a Black Mariah!' To which the eleven year old replied, 'Oh aye, who's she?'

She then settled back into the canvas seat and lit a Park Drive to 'settle her nerves'.

One popular inclusion on a kid's holiday menu was a ride on the donkeys. I always remember they never looked happy and I am not surprised. Having a seven year old porker from Wallasey put on your back determined to kick the hell out of you must have been no fun at all. Located on the sands between central and south piers were donkeys supervised by an unkempt and humourless man. He always looked as though he had just crawled out of bed. His donkeys were huddled together tied in a line. My dad would joke,

'We won't have the one at the end pal, 'cos the rest of 'em'll fall over!'

The melancholy man ignored my dad and simply took his sixpence.

Each afternoon, cries of 'That's the way to do it!' rang across the golden sands. Mr Punch's thrice daily job description would include thrashing his wife, battering a policeman and pummelling a crocodile. Both children and their parents would chuckle at Punch's psychopathic assaults and then engage in repetitive banter:

Mr Punch: 'Oh, yes he is!'

Crowd: 'Oh, no he isn't!'

Hardly Shakespeare I know but such antics were crowd-pulling performances.

The large Woolworths store on the sea front sold everything for your beach experience. You could purchase buckets and spades and paper flags for your sandcastles. Windmills on sticks were guaranteed to turn in the on shore breezes. Plastic starfish moulds and beach balls sat alongside along side cowboy hats, all waiting for a jolly time on the sands.

'Let's bury dad' has always been a popular seashore pastime. You would find hundreds of heads peering just above the sand line, their bodies being patted down and bruised by over-zealous spade-wielding offspring. Youngsters would shiver after emerging from a sub zero dip in the Irish Sea, the white pallor of their skin now changed to an unhealthy blue. Teeth would chatter as they hid behind their towels and attempted to remove stone cold swimming costumes. It was all great fun and such hypothermia merely added to the enjoyment of your Blackpool holiday.

Taking a ride on a green and cream tram from Squires Gate to exotic parts such as Bispham and Thornton Cleveleys was a must.

Clanking noises and the siren bells seemed to mollify discomfort from slatted wooden seats. Double decker trams would give you a better view of such enchanting places as the Pleasure Beach, the Golden Mile, the Tower and Tussauds Waxworks. The Tower and its wonderful ballroom was the place to be, especially when the iconic Reginald Dixon emerged from the depths and played his magnificent Wurlitzer organ. Couples would Military Two Step and Slow Foxtrot to his sonorous melodies. Timorous aunties, now fuelled by port and lemon, dragged their reluctant nephews onto the dance floor. It was all quite embarrassing but the grown ups thought it a great night out.

The Tower had its own menagerie whose tigers and elephants provided the cabaret for the Tower Circus. Charlie Cairoli had us all roaring with laughter as he pretended to throw water over a horrified audience, only to shower them with bits of paper. Trapeze artists gave you a stiff neck and defied gravity as they swung aloft. Acrobats from Dalmatia built human pyramids while uttering unintelligible sounds which gave drama to their act.

An aquarium also helped kids pass some time in particularly inclement weather. The lift to the top of the Tower was always full and echoed with familiar parental remarks such as 'People look like ants, don't they Gerald!' and 'On a clear day ya can see th'Isle o'Man, Beryl!'

Blackpool's three piers boasted stars such as Edmund Hockridge, Jill Day, Stan Stennett and Alma Cogan. Kids and their dads went crabbing over the side of the pier. Some more knowledgeable anglers fished for dabs and pouting using rods with a clothes peg and bell attached to herald their catch. The Metropole Hotel, owned by the Butlin organisation, was regarded by regular Butlin patrons as being up market because it served high tea.

Derby Baths was a colossal building whose brickwork seemed to go on forever. It was known for its Olympic-sized swimming pool and also for its diving board, the platform of which finished just south of the planet Mars. On your ride towards Fleetwood you would pass a magnificent landmark: the Miners' Convalescent Home. On a sunny day its residents would sit out in the front grounds and inhale the fresh air their lungs had been denied for over forty years. It seemed to me shameful and ridiculous compensation for the job's legacy of emphysema and pneumoconiosis.

One of the favourite places to be in Blackpool was the Pleasure Beach. A sign just outside its premises, carrying alliteration worthy of Leonard Sachs, boldly proclaimed, 'Welcome to The Pleasure Beach, A Rip Roaring Riot of Relaxing Revelry'. Rides such as the roller coaster, known as the Big Dipper, rallied your adrenaline as you suddenly changed altitude and then accelerated like a rocket. The Grand National ride too raised your blood pressure and made you aware of G-forces and Newton's laws. Two Ferris wheels, situated side by side, both described circles but in opposite directions. For tiny tots there was the Safari ride. Sideshows offered a coconut shy where frustrated uncles would claim that coconuts were glued in place. Rifle ranges, whose guns fired either corks or pellets, asked you to knock down packets of liquorice allsorts or rows of metal figures. Hook a Duck gave a prize every time unless you suffered from alcoholism. 'Ya can 'ave any prize ya want cock, as long as it's from that shelf!' cried the portly stall-holder. The trouble was, the prize you really wanted was on another shelf and would cost another four goes. The gift usually finished up paying for itself. Rides such as the Parachute, the Aeroplanes and the Mixer were all guaranteed to put into question how well your stomach was able to hold on to your fish and chips.

There is a paradox in a fun park. Should you fall over, you burst out laughing. Do this on the pavement outside, then laughter is never your response. A prime example of such absurdity could always be witnessed in the Fun House. Even as you were queueing to enter its premises a laughing automaton clown rolling backwards and forwards in his glass case had you in hysterics. Once inside the building a rotating barrel would throw you to the ground and churn you around like a cement mixer. Both you and its other passengers would find this amusing. Laughter seemed to numb the discomfort. Similarly, round spinning footplates would throw you off balance and make you desperately lunge for a handrail and giggle your way to safety. Oscillating walkways would slow everyone's pace and women's skirts would be blown above their heads by a shaft compressed air. The bizarre thing about receiving such trauma was that it made you want to go back for a second helping, and subsequently laugh once more at your repeated misfortune.

The slide in the Fun House was a sheer drop and was a sensation similar to hurling yourself off the Eiffel Tower. Friction burns from this structure were common but seemed to make you want to go back and add to your collection. The Hall of Mirrors would make thin ladies fat and fat ladies fatter. Tiny tots would become giants and your six-foot uncle Cyril would turn into a Lilliputian.

I also recall being dragged along to the open-air swimming pool to watch the Miss Blackpool Competition, judged by a celebrity who was currently working on North Pier. A parade of hopefuls, some with skin white enough to give you snow blindness and others with legs bearing a tint of gravy browning, dreamed of stardom. Hour glass figures shared the platform with those not so blessed.

'Number 25 should have stopped at home,' whispered my gran. Old ladies can never whisper and this comment was quite audible, even to number 25 herself. Lecherous men moved their denture plates back and forth and leered at these number-carrying nubile starlets. Even at the age of nine I had reservations about the ethical nature of this showbiz pageant.

If you wanted entertainment in the fifties then Blackpool had something for everyone. A week's half board with decent meals and bracing sea air that was supposed to be good for acne should have been on every GPs prescription pad. Blackpool never failed to disappoint. If you were fortunate enough to meet a gentleman strolling along the prom and you were to say to him, 'You are Lobby Lud of the *Daily Mail* and I claim my five pounds,' then as long as you were carrying that newspaper, you would have enough money to return in September for the Illuminations. Blackpool really did have everything.

Season's greetings

I NEVER KNEW MY DAD. He died when I was two. I knew what he looked like because there was a photograph of him and my mum on the mantelpiece, taken at Rhyl in 1946. I also had another keepsake, his army greatcoat, which we used as an eiderdown in the winter months.

Getting ready for bed in these cold times took place downstairs, in front of the fire, followed by a quick run up to my bedroom. Its cold lino floor forced me to take as few steps as possible, culminating in an athletic leap that would see me hit the mattress with such force that the bedsprings would complain, issuing a discordant welcome. Winter nights in houses like ours saw frost settling on the inside of windows and fires were only lit in your bedroom if you were ill.

Pulling dad's greatcoat on top of me was not easy. It was so heavy, and once under its weave you felt pinned down in a body press by a corpulent wrestler. The coat was warm though, and I could still smell his Brylcreem on its collar.

Tonight's bedtime preparations took longer than usual. It was Christmas Eve and my mother let me stay up later. One of her nylons made do as my Christmas stocking which I had to hang over the back of a chair, secured in place by a huge bulldog clip that took vast amounts of muscle power to prise open. A pillowcase was left on the table for Santa to stuff with presents and then to be placed at the bottom of my bed. A carrot for his reindeer, a glass of sherry and a mince pie completed his needs. It was always a glass of milk for the great man in Mrs Baldock's house, for she hoped he would share her temperance.

I was so excited I thought I would never go to sleep. Indeed, I wanted to stay awake and hear Father Christmas come into my room. I never managed it, not once, for at some stage in the vigil my eyes would close denying me contact with this venerable soul. An easy way of telling if he'd paid me a visit in this darkness, and without me getting cold, was to push my feet to the bottom of the bed. I would then gently probe the bed sheets with my toes and slowly move them from one side of the bed to the other. Such an exploratory manoeuvre was done with the sensitivity and skill of a bomb disposal officer. The discovery of a hard object that crackled as I persisted with these explorations meant only one thing ... wrapping paper, and he'd been!

People started preparing for Christmas in early December, unlike today when as soon as the last egg is consumed on Easter Monday, shops host shelves of selection boxes, crackers and fairy lights. At primary school we made Christmas cards and model Father Christmases. A formula of cotton wool, glue, glitter, scissors, stencils and crepe paper allowed you to construct almost anything. Cotton wool and glue stuck to your skin and pullovers. By the end of the day my mate Henry Bradshaw looked as though he was decomposing and covered in a carpet of white fungus. Patrick Mulvaney had more glitter on his jacket than Liberace and Wallace Pickersgill had to be unstuck from his chair

One thing at primary school that told you Christmas was definitely on its way was the nativity play. Costumes ranged from dyed bed sheets to tea towels and stick on beards. Everyone wanted a beard, even the girls, and most boys refused to perform unless they had a sword. Gold, frankincense and myrrh were someone's vases and bowls from a sideboard. It was ironic that the boy who played Melchior, one of the esteemed wise men, had difficulty with *Janet and John – Book One* and still wet himself. Jasmine Golightly was an overpowering top junior girl who boomed the Virgin Mary's lines like Peggy Mount. Stefan Urbanowicz's dog, Rex, whose coat was white, always deputised as a sheep. Maud Turner's wings, as the arch angel Gabriel, refused to stay on unless she wore her dad's braces outside her white surplice, making her look like an avian Andy Capp. Nine year old Solly Lieberman joked there WAS room at the inn but only if Joseph would give him ten shekels. However, the Christmas message got through and we would finish the day with party games such as musical chairs, oranges and lemons and blind man's buff.

Writing to Father Christmas was another undertaking during mid December. I was always rather careful about my request for presents, mainly because my mother checked the invoice and would tell me off if I was too optimistic. My next-door-neighbour, Linda Baker, had a want list the length of a toilet roll and the man himself would have suffered exhaustion catering for her. I never remembered asking for a tangerine, an apple and a bag of chocolate money to be in my stocking but they were always there.

To communicate with Father Christmas 'in vivo' meant one of your parents taking you to town, and visiting a large department store such as Kendal Milne or Lewis's in Manchester. Even at the age of six, I wasn't sure about this encounter. Younger kids would bawl, some would collapse in tears and some would escape their parent's grip and 'leg it' down the escalator at the sight of this white-haired icon.

Sitting on the old man's knee was uneasy for me too. I would look at his beard, which was starting to yellow from years of use. His conversation was seasoned with the aroma of Player's Navy Cut and I could see a Marks and Spencer shirt collar protruding from underneath his rich red cape. An Ingersoll wristwatch also completed my doubts about this impostor. Queuing for hours to go into Santa's grotto with its warm lighting, enchanting scenery and stuffed reindeer was made worthwhile by the customary present given to you from one of two sacks. This was usually a strip of poorly moulded plastic soldiers wrapped up in festive paper for the boys, while the girls received some plastic jewellery. One year, everyone got a colouring book. The disappointment and anticlimax was so powerful for one lad from Collyhurst that he told Santa's elf, using easy to understand practical terminology, exactly where she could place it.

It was customary to exhume Christmas decorations stored in an old cardboard box. Some paper garlands had clearly overstayed their welcome and disintegrated as we drawing-pinned them to the picture rail. Bits of tinsel seemed to have 'gone off', now lacking lustre and sparkle. Nevertheless, in these times of penury, the motto for most families was to 'make do and mend', and that the show had to go on.

Paper chains and streamers would be tied to the central light fitting and sag across the room before being nailed to the walls. This made the ceiling height lower and your living room now resembled the inside of a Bedouin tent, forcing my lanky mate Jezz to enter with the walk of Groucho Marx.

Balloon blowing time was always worth waiting for. Considering Salford had one of the UK's highest incidence of bronchitis, perhaps second only to Glasgow, most balloons were filled with a mixture of air, smoke from Capstan Full Strength and halitosis. Many of the early inflated ones lost their wind and looked like shrivelled carrots by Christmas Eve. My uncle Ged would attack inflation of these rubber decorations with the determination of one of the Montgolfier brothers. Just as his respiratory efforts had reached a crescendo and the balloon was full, he would proceed to burst it, by insisting on tying the rubber knot with a cigarette in his hand.

Sprigs of mistletoe, along with many of the Christmas presents, were bought on Salford market. Barmy Mick, a hugely popular market trader would insist he was 'giving' his wares away. He had the patter of Max Miller and could work any crowd.

'How about a pair of porcelain cats, ladies?' I once heard him ask, 'Lovely Christmas present, dear. No they're not mounted, just lookin' fondly at each other, love!' His audience would roar with laughter.

I can remember our Christmas tree made from a wire. Branches were tightly wrapped in dark green shiny paper to simulate pine needles. In its raw undecorated state it looked like a prolapsed giant lavatory brush but when festooned with tinsel, baubles and the customary fairy at the top it looked less hideous. The occasional bag of chocolate money and paper stars would hang from its branches, and the final *piece de resistance* was a set of wax candles that we would secure to its branches with crocodile clip candleholders. Once lit, we seemed to ignore the fact that the tree was listing to one side.

With the room lights turned off, it was indeed a joyous thing to behold. In common with most families who possessed such tree decorations the inevitable fire would occur. Although no one left the room whilst the candles were burning, as the festive evening progressed conversations and vigils became less tree-focused. It was usually my gran who would sound the alarm.

'Eh up! Ruddy tree's on fire!' she'd shout, not making any attempt to get out of her armchair and refusing to put down her Mackeson. We had been blissfully unaware that for the past few minutes the back of the fairy's dress was receiving a roasting from beneath. Bags of chocolate money suffered instant devaluation as their molten contents dripped onto the lametta below. The saucepan of water we were urged to keep alongside our tree now extinguished the conflagration and the singed fairy, now with third degree burns, gazed down on us with sadness and despair. Our tree, still smouldering, was now black and charred, resembling a victim of a nuclear attack.

About one week before Christmas Day, carol singers would appear on our streets. Roasted chestnut vendors too were pleasing additions to cold, damp pavements. I remember burning my fingers trying to remove the shell of these red-hot morsels. There was often a man with his barrel organ and pet monkey. Such wildlife fascinated us kids. The only strange fauna we had seen in Salford streets was when Alec Benson treated the coat of his Alsatian dog with peroxide.

The Salvation Army band would gather on Broad Street and this tuneful brass ensemble would herald the coming of the holy time. Silent Night, a carol that my gran claimed always brought a lump to her throat, slowly suffused the city's cold night air. One year she swallowed a large roast chestnut that refused to go down, giving her a similar sensation. Mr Tattersall, a commercial traveller from Fitzwarren Street, joked that when he visited Didsbury 'it was so posh 'round there, the Salvation Army band had its own string section'.

It soon occurred to me and my mates that carol singing could prove to be a lucrative venture. The trouble was, we only knew one carol and indeed, only one of its verses. Armed with this narrow repertoire of song we set about fleecing the local community with a rendition of the Bohemian carol Good King Wenceslas. Raymond Cardwell was the loudest of our quartet and would insist on singing 'Good King Wences Last Looked Out'. We were doing well – a penny a house in George Street. Despite the occasional unpleasant advice from some residents, which usually was something to do with urination and travel, the night's attempt at being choristers was successful and gave us all enough money for penny Spanish, flying saucers and a gobstopper.

As I advanced in years and Father Christmas became less of a credible figure I would search the house for presents when my

mother left for work. Favourite and easily detectable hiding places were the back of the wardrobe or even on top of it. Under my mum's bed was another. My mate Jezz said his parents would hide his stuff in the loft, a place inaccessible for him but sadly not for Dermot Hooley. Terraced houses had a common loft space that ran the entire length of the row. The Hooley family, of which there were eight in number, lived in an end of terrace on Jezz's row. They were an unpleasant group, of whom Jezz's dad once said, 'They'd pinch the air you breathe, that lot!' He was, in fact correct; Dermot liberated from Jezz's loft, an Airfix Wellington bomber kit, an Alan Ladd repeater rifle and his sister's Marmet doll's pram. The Hooleys regularly featured on the calling cards of Salford City Police.

Most kids were up early on Christmas morning attacking wrapping paper with a frenzied determination. Many parents would insist they only opened one present and keep the rest for after Christmas dinner. Sometimes the wait was too much and bits were torn from around the edges of the parcel in an attempt to see inside.

'Now do that again our Tony, and yer'll get nowt!' The eight year old then reluctantly ceased his examination.

If you were allowed outside in the morning you would see kids on bicycles (usually second hand), girls with doll's prams or roller skates, lads wearing Davy Crockett hats and tiny tots pushing toy Matchbox cars. It was a time of great excitement. Christmas dinner was always at one o'clock, allowing time for churchgoers to have completed their worship, though many would have been to midnight mass.

We usually had people round for dinner, namely those who were too old to cook and could do nothing else but sit on chairs. They were the ones who bought you practical gifts like socks, gloves and handkerchiefs. Other distant relatives sent you money. Auntie Doreen knitted me a pullover one year that made me look particularly camp. My mother's enthusiasm didn't help,

'Oooh, Doreen! That's just what he wanted. Thanks love. Now, what do you say to Auntie Doreen, chuck?' I knew what I wanted to say but I had to be polite.

Mrs Eckersley, a widow in her eighties, was a regular name on our guest list. She was a delightful lady who would sit on the sofa showing everyone her capacious pink bloomers whose elastic finished just above her knees. She was the doyen of malapropisms.

'I've knitted him one of those balalaikas, Mavis. Keep his little 'ead warm.'

The meal table had two cloths spread across it and included the kitchen table acting as an extension. Seating was always a problem. Two tea chests with a plank spanning them could hold three bottoms, though only two if my giant amoeba of a cousin Thomas was visiting. Chairs of different sizes were placed in no particular order around the table and when the clientele were all seated I would gaze across at the shapes opposite, their contours resembling a New York City skyline. For parties we would often borrow the wooden form (bench) from the chippie in Croft Street.

Crackers were pulled and the usual plastic toy, paper hat and riddle would tumble from its cardboard roll. My favourite riddle was:

Q: 'What disease do you get from Xmas decorations?'

A: 'Tinselitis!'

Hardly Abbott and Costello I know, but what do you expect from Woolworth's crackers at one and six a box?

There were no 'starters' in our house for Christmas dinner, though one year my mum baked a Yorkshire pudding the size of the pitch at Old Trafford. We all doused this baked batter with thick gravy before the main meal. Aperitifs took the form of sherry, milk stout or a glass of Wilson's bitter. Uncle Des had never married and was a whisky man. You could tell. His varicose and bulbous nose protruded from a face flanked by red and inflamed cheeks. His eyes hosted a network of scarlet lines running across an almost yellow surface. He was certainly no Cary Grant and nobody went anywhere near the mistletoe when he was in the vicinity. However, he was a kind and generous man whose benevolence regarding gifts and pocket money was always in direct proportion to his blood alcohol level.

Chicken, sprouts, carrots, peas and roast potatoes constituted the *plat du jour*, followed by plum pudding, and custard to die for. Sometimes there was no custard and Carnation milk was its poor substitute.

'Yer've not put a thre'p'nny bit in it this year 'ave ya mother?' shouted Doreen, 'I cracked me bloomin' false teeth on one o' those last year.'

I never had turkey for Christmas until I was in my early twenties. A goose in our street was unheard of. Uncle Des would buy the bird and drop it round on Christmas Eve. Once he told me he was short of money and that in October we should buy our budgie a pair of chest expanders and hope for the best. Remember, these were the days when a Big Mac was something my granddad would wear when it was raining and crisps were one flavour only. They were simple times, but happy times.

Our Christmas cake would boast an off-white snowman, standing alone and making a miserable figure on a carpet of icing. My mother's icing would have given mining engineers a problem. However, when this unyielding mass was cracked open with a knife the size of a machete, it would give you enough glucose for a year. Underneath this solidified sugar lay a mixture of marzipan, currants, raisins, sultanas and mixed spice all soaked in brandy. We always kept a small bottle of this spirit in the pantry for medicinal purposes and for mixing the Christmas cake filling. I never realised how therapeutic brandy was until my gran revealed the ailments it relieved, ranging from curing her 'bad heart' to 'settling her nerves'.

I was always eager to go out to play in the time remaining before it went dark. This wish was denied and I would have to wait until Boxing Day morning. After the Queen's speech at 3 o'clock, uncle Des would have dropped off on the sofa, his snoring matched by Mrs Eckersley's own nasal harmonics. The noises emanating from the duo sounded like someone ripping up old lino. When they did recover from their comas it was time to get out the board games. Waddington's Monopoly was a favourite and gave us impossible aspirations of owning properties on Bond Street. The wealthiest I ever became was to own the water works and my 'Get Out of Jail' card. My mum jokingly said she would send it to the Hooleys.

One year my cousin Thomas was bought the game Escalado. This was essentially a plastic mat that vibrated when you turned a handle at one end. Onto the mat you placed metal horses complete with their jockeys. The trembling mat made these horses move forward towards a finishing post at the opposite end of the sheet. It was a game that adults enjoyed by having penny bets on which of these visibly rabid horses would finish first.

Though we never had very much money, there never seemed to be a shortage of food on this day. Guests would always bring things such as mince pies and fancies. Nuts appeared from nowhere and the lino was peppered with walnut shells. Hardest of all were the Brazil nuts. You needed the physique of Tarzan to crack them open.

I got into trouble by cracking them in the space between the door and door-frame and unfortunately cracked not just the nuts but the door architrave. Christmas tea-time meant sandwiches and sausage rolls followed by blancmange as pink as a baby's cheeks. Tinned pineapple chunks and evaporated milk would sometimes appear and this festive *repas* was finished off with yet another slice of Christmas cake.

Party games were played until late. 'Consequences' was an amusing game where you wrote down sentences about questions you were asked and then passed them on to the person on your right. The exercise always produced bizarre stories. One example from our family of wordsmiths read:

'Uncle Des met The Queen at Old Trafford, and she said to him, "How about a bit?"

And he said to her, "Can I have custard with it?"

And, the consequence was, he turned into a frog and she got a pan of chips on.'

After a few port and lemons the ladies would roar with laughter. Indeed, Mrs Eckersley, on her way home, would quip, 'I laughed so much I thought my bloomers would never dry! He's a real card is yer uncle Des.'

I feel 'saddo' was a more apt description.

Pass the parcel in our house was a real favourite, though perhaps not at the Crawshaw residence in Florin Street. Mrs Crawshaw was a Communist and pragmatist to say the least. She had more kids than teeth and brought her kids up to know what life really was all about. Their parcel game would conclude with a sheet of empty paper and her comment, 'Disappointed? Well, that's what life's like kids, so get used to it!'

The Anderton family next door had a piano in their parlour, and on occasions we would be invited in for a sing-song. This was very boring for us kids but the grown ups loved it. Tear jerkers such as 'We'll meet again' and 'Roses of Picardy' would always be emotional, particularly for my gran and Mrs Eckersley, having lost husbands and sons in both World Wars.

At an unbelievably late hour I would be packed off to bed with an assurance that I could put on my playing out clothes in the morning for a couple of hours before I would be scrubbed senseless, ready for an evening visit to my Auntie Eileen's in Eccles, to complete the Boxing Day celebrations. According to my mum, they had a few bob and I was told to be on my best behaviour. My gran accused them of having more money than sense, simply because they possessed a Flatley washing machine. Activities with the adults were the same each year. Story telling, party songs and games, as predictable as ever. The doleful sight of my uncle Des, ever the optimist, standing alone and unloved, under the mistletoe, concluded the yuletide activities.

Charlie

THE YEAR 1896 SAW OSCAR WILDE imprisoned in Reading gaol. Gold was first discovered in the rocky metamorphic seams of the Klondike, and curiously enough, the first speeding ticket was issued to an over-zealous Kent motorist caught doing 8mph. The tenth of December that year marked the death of Alfred Nobel, Swedish chemist and inventor of gunpowder. The future sinister applications of his work on this explosive led to the establishment of the peace prize carrying his name.

It was also during that month, in the Lancashire town of Leigh, my granddad Charles Harold Swift was born. Charlie was one of eight children, the boys all destined for work in the local collieries, whose principal job was to furnish huge tonnages of coal to feed the boilers of the Lancashire cotton mills. Two of them never reached the school leaving age of twelve, one succumbing to septicaemia while the other drowned in the nearby Bridgewater canal.

The start of the Great War saw many of Charlie's school pals enlist, destined for combat in Belgium and northern France. His regiment, The Lancashire Fusiliers, played a significant role in Gallipoli and twenty year old Charlie lost part of an ear at Sulva Bay, whilst coming under fire wading ashore to the beaches. While his mates who fought in the fields of Flanders fell victim to trench foot and typhus, Charlie's battalion was exposed to mosquitoes, vectors of malaria, a disease endemic in that foreign land. Prior to this bloody conflict, most people living in the UK believed an Ottoman to be a piece of wooden furniture used as a footstool or for storing linen. Being told that his Kitchener Volunteers battalion of the Lancashire Fusiliers were off to fight the Ottomans must have been confusing for them all. Following his Dardanelles experience, and by the end of 1918, he had survived further action on the western front.

In the post-war period of 1919 to 1932 Charlie worked as a coal miner at the Moseley colliery near his home-town of Leigh, before transferring to Agecroft pit. During this time he met and married my grandmother. This was my gran's second husband. Her first was my father's dad, corporal William Carline of the Northumberland Fusiliers, killed in action at the Battle of Passchendaele. The closure of the pit in 1932 led Charlie to seek alternative employment at Tom Cussons's soap factory in Kersal Vale. 'Soapy Tom's', as it was known to us kids, became an employer of a large workforce at that time.

For much of my infancy I was looked after during working hours by my gran, Charlie's wife. My mother was manageress of the UCP tripe shop on Broad Street, Pendleton, and worked long hours. As a toddler, and to prevent me from 'toddling' too far, my gran would place three cushions on the floor of the dolly tub and deposit me in there whilst she completed her daily chores. Her invention was the prototype of the modern day play pens but the contraption would have failed to secure today's kite mark. Both Amnesty International and The European Court on Human Rights today would have opposed its use. I can still recall staring at the walls of that washtub, complete with its three hundred and sixty degree grey, galvanised vista. According to my wife, the number of times I banged my head against its metal wall accounts for my adult psychological makeup. I would occasionally look up to see my gran and her visitors staring down at me as though I was some freshly caught Old World primate on show at the fair.

On occasions I would be released from my cell and would crawl around the flagged floor of the living room. When I looked up towards the ceiling I could see the wooden clothes rack hanging from metal brackets designed to dry and aerate the washing. It worked on a pulley system and could be raised and lowered. When I was older and more mischievous I remember pulling its rope so hard the contraption shot upwards with such force it cracked all the plaster in the ceiling. A clout from Charlie was my wages for that piece of experimentation. I also received another hefty thrashing from Charlie when I'd been in such a rush to go out to play. I hadn't fastened its rope tight enough to the cleat on the wall. The contraption suddenly decided to release itself and let gravity do the rest. Unfortunately, Charlie, seated by the fire in his wooden rocking chair, was directly underneath its flight path and remained dizzy and bruised for two days. He can't have been that badly injured because the whacks he administered really hurt!

The mantelpiece above the black cast iron oven and fire grate showed a sepia picture of the happy couple taken about three years after they had married. Perhaps the term 'happy couple' didn't quite fit, since along with all family photographs of that time, everyone looked as miserable as sin. The man would stand alongside his seated wife, him in his only best suit, and she in her only best dress. Perhaps cheese hadn't been invented in those times, hence the doleful expressions on their faces. Even photographs of their kids reflected images of youngsters who looked as they were about to be shot.

Charlie loved his pipe. In fact, he had two of them. Both were kept on the mantelpiece alongside a small jam jar that housed his paper spills for lighting them. As a young lad I would help him roll them; one tightly rolled spill would last him three or four smokes. I could never understand why Charlie smoked. Throughout his days as a miner he must have inhaled incredible amounts of carbon in the form of coal dust. Indeed, should Charlie's skeleton ever be unearthed in thousands of years time they would have no difficulty whatsoever in carbon dating him.

The tobacco he used was called Twist and looked like a piece of old, black rope. He would take a penknife from his waist-coat pocket and cut a small segment of this tobacco and then proceed to roll it up in his hands to release the dried leaf fibres. His right index finger would then push this mass into the bowl of the pipe to pack it down. The knack was to gauge enough air space within this bolus to allow the pipe to draw. A lighted spill, together with curious facial antics, would together set fire to leafy fuel. I would watch this refined procedure and wait for him to push his bloodshot cheeks in and out like fervid bellows. The smoke would then appear from within the pipe and then his mouth, spitting out wreaths of acrid smog. These contortions would speed up until flames too shot into the air, completing the combustion process. His final action before sitting back in his rocking chair was to stick his finger into the burning cauldron to pack down the 'baccy'. The digit he used was constantly charred from years of this habit. His visits to the tobacconist would also include purchasing seven penn'orth of Irish. This was nicotine-based snuff, and was the Victorians' first attempts at snorting stimulants, soon to be followed by powdered cocaine.

Charlie was a creature of habit. Each evening he would sit on the same chair exactly the same distance away from the fire. The ceiling above his head bore a dark brown, resinous pigmentation as the tobacco smoke rose and then condensed on the surface of the plaster. The smoke was a revolting smell and one so concentrated it could have fumigated the whole of Kew gardens. Then, when you weren't expecting it, Charlie would raise the corner of his mouth and, with an action worthy of a cobra, spit a jet of sputum into the fire. On occasions the tar-laden saliva would settle on the grate and sizzle for a few seconds before dying in the heat. Charlie was not a person who showed great affection for anything other than his pipe. The odd time he did put me on his knee I was glad to be returned to the floor. His breath often stank of tar residue mixed with putrefying black pudding. That breath, if bottled, would have cleared the trenches of the western front years earlier. Did my gran, whom he always referred to as 'mother', ever let him kiss her?

Charlie had a penchant for pobs. This food was essentially bits of bread plucked from a loaf and soaked in warm milk. A spoon full of sugar completed the dish and he would consume this delicacy with supping noises as he drew this mash into his mouth. His hand would then be drawn across his lips to remove milk and bread debris. This lack of dining etiquette was further enhanced by a belch, upon which he would thump his chest and say 'Manners!' I suppose this was his way of repenting for his lack of social graces and having the eating habits of a bulldog. Any spillages from his spoon or bowl would settle on the oil-cloth of the wooden table and then be wiped clean by my gran. Indeed, my gran, like most housewives of that time, waited on her man, kept the house in good order and looked after the kids. My mother would quip that Charlie was a considerate man in that he would open the back door for my gran as she brought the heavy bucket of coal indoors.

Such a Victorian mindset could also be found when Charlie had his bath. Now, this performance could easily have been an extension of Charlie's days as a miner. The tin bath was placed in front of the fire and my gran would fill the thing with hot water from the copper in the kitchen. Charlie would strip and then climb into the metal tub. He was naked, apart from his cap and pipe. These were only removed when my gran poured water over his head to wash his hair. He would grasp the pink carbolic soap and flannel, then wash his arms, legs and torso. My gran would complete his dip by scrubbing his back. Charlie would then stand up and be given a starched white towel to dry himself.

Charlie always wore combinations as his underwear. He would even have done so during a mid-day stroll in Death Valley. The garment's leggings finished just above his ankles. The vest section had three buttons, which, I suppose, were to increase or reduce ventilation to his chest. His woollen trousers would have been the envy of Simon Cowell, and started just below the nipple line. The expression 'getting a belt round the ears' very nearly applied literally when you saw the position of Charlie's kecks. He always had a patch in the crotch of his trousers, neatly sewn in place by my gran. Uncle Tommy reckoned he had turbo flatulence, hence the need for repair. In the summer, Charlie would acknowledge the heat by not wearing a shirt, but putting his braces over his combinations. I once observed him getting ready to visit his sister one Sunday afternoon. His, shiny shirt collar was separate from his shirt. A brass collar stud was then used to secure it in place. His shirt collars were so starched it was a wonder he didn't decapitate himself as he turned his head. His big, black boots would shine in the seldom-seen Salford sun.

Were a clinical psychologist ever to have examined Charlie, they would have labelled his psychological profile as being a 'miserable old bugger'. I never saw him smile and only once did I hear him say something witty. One evening I saw him stand in front of the mirror with his eyes closed.

'What are you doing granddad?' I enquired.

''am seein' worr I look like when 'am asleep,' he replied. Hardly Tommy Trinder material, I know but that was the best you got. His face could be best described as seamed, rather like the coal he once mined. The surface of his skin showed lines of thin, red blood vessels desperate to escape injury from their daily scrape with his cut-throat razor. His morning face shone from both wash and shaving soap. His evening skin was bristly, hard stubble and its touch could have planed wood. Charlie's hands had a surface like the bark of an oak tree and were seasoned from years of hard manual work. When Charlie looked at you his rheumy, tired eyes revealed little emotion. These were eyes that in their youth had witnessed carnage and inhumanity on an unimaginable scale. They had hardship and poverty etched into them.

Observing Charlie without his cap was quite an extraordinary experience. It was the most hideous haircut I'd ever seen, almost as though the barber bore him a grudge. The final tonsorial effect made him look like an escaped Victorian psychiatric patient, and not all there. I would go with him to get a haircut and the barber must surely have been a retired sheep shearer. Out would come the shears, straight up the back of his neck and then scissors would leave a tuft of sad and lonely looking hair on top. At the age of five I witnessed the final episode of this barber's technique when he appeared to set Charlie alight. A lighted wax taper was played around Charlie's neck and ears with the rhythmic movements of a fire-eater. The singeing process burned off excess stubble and you could smell burning hair. On one occasion you could also smell burning flesh when the barber turned to answer a customer's question.

My gran was a former cotton mill worker. The legacy of her trade was that she was quite deaf and, therefore, skilled at lip-reading. She would also shout at you when she spoke, a habit once more gained from the constant loudness of the cotton looms. However, I never saw her shout at Charlie; in fact, they didn't talk much to each other at all. Their lives were set in a routine, and things just seemed to happen with a repetitive predictability. It was as though both of them had turned on the auto-pilot.

Gran wore a shawl over her pinny and clogs on her feet. She had been prescribed wire-rimmed spectacles that she always wore, unlike her husband. Charlie's reason for not wearing these accessories was 'I don't hold wi' 'em!' He was also stubborn about taking medication.

'A dose o'pink, if 'am not reglar! That's it!' he would say to his wife. 'Pink' was the name given to a brand of opening medicine or laxative. 'Aye, that stuff gets a road through ya.' It was unfortunate that a dose of 'Pink' failed to touch the bout of bronchitis he suffered in the winter of 1961, which then developed into full-blown pneumonia. The local GP, Dr Boothroyd, diagnosed the worst and he was admitted to Crumpsall hospital. Charlie, at the age of 65, passed away two days later.

'I knew he were bad [unwell]', said Mrs Gomersall, who lived next door. 'He'd not touched his pipe for days'.

His beloved rocking chair remained a lonely sight in the living room from that day onwards. His two pipes were placed on top of his cap and laid on the seat. Charlie was cremated and his ashes found themselves in an urn on the windowsill of the parlour, next to the aspidistra. Charlie had a predilection for iron-rich black puddings which led him to consume one a day for over thirty years. The cremation procedure thus prescribed for Charlie would have been similar to smelting in a blast furnace. No wonder his urn weighed a ton!

Can your Ronnie come out to play?

THEY WERE ALWAYS EASY TO WIND UP. Sure as eggs. Several wisely chosen words and they'd pop, like a cork from a champagne bottle. They never caught us, because the thing about park keepers – or 'parkies' as we called them – was that they all had a limp. It was a prerequisite for the job. A limp and a waddle, they all had them. It amused us even more when they tried to chase us and increase their speed into a gallop. Inevitably, their cap would fall off and they'd run out of puff. Such lack of oxygen meant they couldn't even blow their whistle. It was like taking sweets from a baby.

'Oi! Gammy leg!'

'Eh! Long John Silver. Can't catch us!'

'Douglas Bader! Where's ya Spitfire!' The insults were endless.

We'd probably visit the park a couple of times a week during the good weather. It was our gang, and we'd make straight for the swings. There were two rows of them and some of us would have first go, whilst the others pushed. You always had to be careful as to who pushed you. If you got Glen Cohen then you enjoyed yourself. Glen's dad was Jewish and a rainproof cloth salesman. His mother was proud of her Highland ancestry and was determined to reflect this heritage in the name of her son. However, should an intruder like Les Batty give you a shove then you were soon to be destined for intensive care. Les had all the personality and social graces of Vlad the Impaler and only ceased his pushes when you were thrown into a tree some hundred yards away. Morris Barlow never needed assistance. He could get up speed and height by jerking his legs back and forth. He was as persistent and determined as a bluebottle against a pane of glass. Then, at the high point of his swing he would deck off and land yards away without falling over. We'd often have decking off competitions and once poor Lenny Beswick landed minus most of his short trousers as they caught and tore in the wooden seat coupling.

Frankie loved to stand on the contraption and gain incredible height as he leaned forward at the start of each swing. It was simple harmonic motion and a truly breath-taking spectacle. Had Frankie passed his eleven plus examination, I am sure he would have realised that trying a full three hundred and sixty degree oscillation was impossible. He got as far as half way round and gravity quickly put paid to achieving the final one hundred and eighty. It happened so quickly too, and was like watching a glider stall. We visited him in Salford Royal Hospital and took him the *Beano* and some Uncle Joe's mint balls.

There were two roundabouts. One was meant for smaller children. It was divided into sections, each with wooden boards as seats, and a platform. If you looked down between the boards, years of litter and detritus had collected there, and you'd see lollipop sticks by the thousand. Les loved this apparatus. He would offer to slowly turn little kids whilst their mothers had a cigarette and a natter. All was well until Les changed from Dr Jeckyll into Mr Hyde. Applying high speed to maximise centrifugal force, he would launch the little'uns into oblivion. Having achieved such genocide, Les would run off, swearing at the traumatised parents, and at the same time giving them his much-favoured two-fingered salute.

For older kids there was the spider's web, a hexagon that spun horizontally on a central pivot. Once more, break-neck speeds could be achieved on this mechanism and it was common to see youngsters hanging on for dear life, completely horizontal. Their feet would describe a huge circle of orbit, whilst their hair would be pushed flat and their cheeks would flap from achieving such G-forces. Many weaker fellows failed to remain attached and soon obeyed the spin drier principle and were flung into distant parts of north Lancashire.

All of the apparatus in this play area was subject to abuse and took health and safety to extremes. The umbrella was yet another device capable of ill treatment. Instead of allowing it to spin gently, many psychopathic playmates would rock it back and forth with such gusto that it often came away from its mountings, felling any onlookers standing within a few yards of the thing.

There were no rubber mats or play bark to cushion a fall. Should you come a cropper and tumble from one of these structures then it was an immediate visit to casualty. Scratched, bleeding knees, contusions and fractures were all in a day's good play on this equipment. The slide, a seemingly benign structure, was responsible for lacerated backsides and third degree burns, particularly if the previous players had polished it beforehand. Joyce Pickles suffered chipped front teeth when she decided to go head first down the slide. Her brother Roger was nearly emasculated when he decided to walk up the slide as Terry Fitzparick was coming down backwards. Going on the slide after it had rained meant you got stuck half way down.

Some say it was safer for kids to play out in the streets in the forties and fifties, and that there were fewer perverts in cars – probably true, but only because there were fewer cars. Play streets were off limits to through traffic but in any street you would witness the usual repertoire of street games. Kids created their own entertainment, whether it was swinging on cast iron lamp-posts on a rope or playing with matchstick boats in the street gutters and puddles. There was always plenty to do. Girls would play two balls against someone's wall and sing 'One, Two, Three O'Leary.'

There was a sudden craze of hula hoops. Most of us lads were appalling exponents of the game. Paula Doherty held master classes, teaching us the technique. We all reckon she'd inherited her pelvic gyrations and thrusts from her mother who used to regularly ply her trade at the bottom of Cross Lane near the docks on a Saturday night. Sandy Krink couldn't afford a hula hoop so he used and old bicycle tyre. Whenever Les Batty visited our street he would spin the tyre around Sandy's neck. The bruising was there for weeks.

Some kids had rather unusual hobbies such as collecting car number plates. Les Batty had a literal take on this and his back yard was full of them. Nobody dared tell him that what you really did was to write down the registration number. The last two letters on

the vehicle index number gave you clues as to where it was from. MN was Manchester and RJ was a Salford plate. We'd also go onto Broad Street and spot the red British Road Services wagons. They bore their depot names on the side of their trailers. We marvelled at their journeys from exotic places such as Mansfield and Worksop and logged them in our notebooks.

A dangerous past-time during the summer months was catching wasps in your handkerchief. There certainly was a knack to being successful at trapping these insects. An old jam jar with some sugar water was placed on the ground and the wasp vigil commenced. As soon as one landed on the jar we would throw the handkerchief over it and then bunch it up to trap the creature. Lifting the cloth to your ear allowed you to hear the annoyed beast buzzing around inside. Some of us were more skilful at this than others. The only successful thing that Walter Kipple had ever achieved in his life was being born. Hence, during the months of July and August his right ear was always twice the size of the other.

Bubble gum was the 'in thing' to chew, giving a trans-Atlantic image and making you look cool. Teddy boys were completely unimpressive without it. However, with us kids, the stuff got everywhere and bubble gum-blowing competitions were the biggest offenders. Following your careful inflation of the gum balloon it would either explode itself or one of your mates would pop it with their fingers. The sticky shrapnel from this detonation would get in your hair, on your eyebrows, up your nose, and if you wore spectacles your vision was gone for a couple of hours until you scraped away the glutinous stuff. Boys would get hard impacted pieces of it on their short trousers and girls would find it in their pig-tails.

During the summer months the pitch from road surfaces stuck to your shoes and often large sheets of it made you look as though you were wearing flippers. The unyielding black stuff got everywhere and you frequently got a whack from your mum as it permanently stained your short trousers or skirt. In the heat it was soft enough to roll beads of it into marbles, leaving your fingers black and stinking of bitumen. Another use of this black stuff was to set fire to it and watch the acrid fumes rise from the road.

A wonderful way of annoying your neighbours was to play 'Robber's Knock' or 'Knock Down Ginger'. This antisocial game varied in its complexity. In simple terms it involved you knocking on someone's door and running away. Old people were easy prey and you gained a macabre pleasure from witnessing them use up the finite amount of energy they had left in their bodies. Getting out of a chair six times and waving a walking stick certainly took years off their allowance.

More complex forms of the game involved much planning and engineering. Tying two or more door-knockers together with a long piece of fishing line produced endless fun as you hid behind a wall. Responding to the knock on the first door, the unsuspecting resident would then trigger knocks on the other doors. It was highly amusing as they all answered knocks at the same time, which subsequently triggered another knock on the first door. Mr Tobias of Florin Street came out of his house with the speed of a gazelle intending to put an end to our enjoyment and sadly garrotted himself on the fishing line, thus muting his cry of 'Come here you little bas…!'

Another good way of harassing a neighbour was to keep kicking your football against the side of their house. This certainly irritated those residents who worked nights, and usually resulted in them issuing us with threats and shouting profanities. Should we ignore their ultimatum and persist with our game, a chase would ensue and poor old Walter, who ran as quickly as a slug with rheumatism, would take the group's cumulative thrashing.

Any place south of Droylsden would have referred to them as marbles. To us in Salford, they were alleys and there were some skilled players amongst our fraternity. Irene Wright had the aim and control of a professional snooker player and had never heard of beta-blockers. She was a great nudger, a move generated by using the broad length of your index finger to move the alley forward. She was, perhaps, most renowned for her flicking dexterity and accuracy. Holding an alley on your index finger and flicking it with your thumb could send the ball a considerable distance at great speed. To her, angles, spins and forces were no problem. To Alec Hardman of Ellor Street, with the hand/eye coordination of a bomb aimer suffering from Saint Vitus Dance, the game continued to be impossible.

There were two types of terrain on which this game could be played. On pavements or hard ground, a chalked circle was drawn into which you nudged your opponent's alley with your own. If you were playing 'keepsy', their glass ball now became yours. On softer ground a hole was dug instead of the chalked circle. Irene could knock alleys everywhere and could even play a profitable game on cobbled streets – now, that *was* control. Small bags of shiny, multicoloured alleys were sold at our local paper shop in John Street. The proprietor, Mrs Ellis, was a jolly yet boring soul. Asking her for a bag of alleys, she would reply:

'Lost yer marbles cock? I lost mine years ago. That's nine pence, love.'

I would look at the glass beads and wonder how they put that spiral drop of paint inside. Some of the colours and shades we had never seen before.

Ask any of us to show you their cache of alleys and you would see an array of action-torn, scratched glass balls. Some were made of white alabaster scarred by months of use. Some kids bounced them on the pavement. Les Batty would often grab some from your bag and throw them at a wall so hard they would shatter. You felt as though you wanted to whack him but innate cowardice prevented us from doing so. Most alley players possessed a 'dobber' that was an oversized alley, well over an inch in diameter. Dobbers were used to try to change the course of a game by knocking away your opponent's threatening glass bead. The dobber was dropped from a height above the field of play and hopefully scattered the balls. Alley laws often varied from street to street. You could use 'Right to Dob' only once per game in our street. However, if psycho Les Batty once more visited our street, to avoid a thump on the ear you let him dob as much as he wanted. Les often used ball bearings he'd stolen from Mather and Platt's iron works.

Marble swapping was a deadly serious business and practised with the negotiation and precision of a narcotics deal. Sandy Krink had a colourful alley of magenta, white and turquoise all spiralled on each other. It was slightly larger than the rest and easier to flick. It cost me fifteen of my own plus two dobbers. Sandy was some businessman and I was some mug.

When the boys in our street were really stuck for something to do, bizarre competitive challenges took place. Wrestling bouts, where you jostled with your opponent whilst seated on someone's shoulders, would usually finish with the unseated candidate tumbling to the ground and dislocating his shoulder. Other pursuits that usually terminated in hospitalisation were seeing who could do backward flips from someone's wall, or have piggy-back races on the ice. Jumping from the Frederick Road bridge onto a partly submerged barge in the Cut Canal frequently resulted in participants swallowing litres of this polluted water. The game of 'Leap Frog' was fine unless you were allocated a mis-match. Bernard Hinkley from Primrose Street had the morphology of a rhino and if poor old Walter Kipple tried to jump over him it was like watching someone with a death wish hurling themselves against the Aswan dam.

My mate Herbie was once taken home by a policeman who proceeded to tell his mother that he'd been found playing inter-street altitudinal urination. The offence was, of course, seeing how high you could wee up a wall. Herbie's mother instantly gave him a clout around the ear, a tearful Herbie admitted to me later:

'I wouldn't mind, but Doreen McClaggen won the competition!'

When playing 'What's The Time Mr Wolf?' it was always dinner time for fifteen-stone Bernard, while it was an impossibility for Lenny Beswick, who could only tell you where the big and little hands of the clock were positioned. Homemade kites constructed from bamboo canes and newspaper rarely gained much lift-off and really hurt when a sudden gust of wind sent them darting back at you. Zeta gliders were fast and extremely dangerous. Should you get in the flight path of these plastic aerofoils it was sudden death. Also if your thumb got in the way as you released its stretched elastic you were minus a thumbnail. Wow, that did hurt!

'Ip, dip, my blue ship, sailing on the water, like a cup and saucer' was an example of a commonly used chant to decide who was going to be chosen for some game. 'One potato, two potato, three potato, four,' was another, along with 'ickle, ockle, chocolate bockle, ickle, ockle out!' There seemed to be a desperate need for a literacy hour in schools even in those days.

Girls played quite happily at hopscotch, on roller skates or played 'five stones' or 'jacks'. However, the most popular game you would find on any street was skipping. Old clothes-lines were tied to the cast iron lamppost and produced hours of pleasure and entertainment. The song or rhyme the girls would sing dictated the skipping manoeuvres. All time favourites included 'Down by the River, Down by the Sea', 'Teddy Bear, Teddy Bear', 'Down in the Valley' and also 'On a Mountain, Stands a Lady'. These games involved tremendous agility, balance and coordination but were too benign for us boys. Any lads who dared participate in skipping were branded homosexual by Les Batty. Mind you, he wouldn't have tried to insult Rocky Marciano as he 'Salt, Mustard, Vinegar and Peppered' his way around the gym.

Giles, however, seemed immune to such derision. He was an extremely talented skipper and was more than a match for the girls. Sadly his skipping days came to an abrupt finish when he joined in with the girls in New Hall Street. They were using a soaking wet lorry rope, which stank of diesel. The thing weighed a ton and took three girls to turn it. Les Batty bullied his way into the game and proceeded to turn the rope at a supersonic speed. Giles managed to keep pace for most of the time but was unfortunately struck on the head by the heavy object and remained concussed for weeks after.

Pea guns, pea shooters, spud guns and catapults were usually the sole property of the boys in the street. One exception was Elsie Fawcett, for she possessed all of the above weaponry, plus a whip and sheath knife. It was always a great comfort knowing Elsie was on your side and even Les Batty said he would sooner have a boil lanced than cross her. One of Elsie's favourite games was doing hand-stands against the wall. It was not a pretty sight as her navy blue knickers, the size of an army surplus parachute, came into view.

'Stop lookin' at me knickers!' she would shout to us boys. That command was easy to obey. Sandy Krink told me many years later that the sight of Elsie's drawers put him off sex for life.

Few youngsters had bicycles which often numbered only one per street. Many adults, however, would use bikes for cycling to work. A favourite past-time of mine and Sandy's was to help Mr Ollerenshaw deliver his boxes of tinned meat and fruit to shops down Ordsall. We sat in the back of his lorry behind long green tarpaulins. Sometimes, as we passed a bloke on his bike, we would lift the covers and shout such witticisms as, 'Get off and milk it!' or 'Hey, mister! Yer wheel's fallin' off!'

I recall one trip when Sandy's remark to an old bloke who was gasping for air whilst pedalling along Cross Lane was a tad OTT.

'Can't yer go any faster, ya cripple?' came the insult, as we overtook the gentleman at twenty miles an hour. Ten seconds later found us stopped at traffic lights and the cyclist had caught us up. The two thumps we got from him showed him to be far from disabled and Mr Ollerenshaw terminated our employment.

An exciting challenge was making 'bogeys' or wooden go-karts, with old pram wheels and wooden planks as the chassis. An old UCP tripe box or wooden vegetable crate acted as the seating compartment. A rope lashed to the axel of the front wheels simulated the steering column. We'd play with these cars for days on end. Bogey racing on the cinder crofts was the next best thing to watching Formula 1. The key to your success lay in the person who pushed you around the course and also how the driver negotiated chicanes and hair-pin bends. Should the driver over-steer on a bend then the wheels locked against the chassis and over they would go. Henry Ford would have been proud of these diminutive auto engineers. Some versions had big pram wheels at the rear, others used similar sized wheels all around. GT models had handbrakes bolted to the seating area and application of these wooden shafts allowed impressive hand-break turns. Obstacle courses made

from old bricks tested the steering capability of these junior Grand Prix aces. Ronnie Price's kart had no limitations and travelled just short of achieving a sonic boom.

Late September saw our principal interest change to conkers. Kids collected so many conkers it was amazing any new Horse Chestnut trees grew. Everyone wanted their conkers tough, hard and able to resist battle fatigue. Sandy soaked his in vinegar, Lenny baked his in the oven, whilst Giles preferred to use nail varnish, some on his nails and some on the conkers. I kept some of mine back from the last year and that seemed to give them a strong and robust property. It was a dangerous sport and injuries ranging from contused knuckles to bruises on the face were frequent misfortunes. Again, the rule was never to play Les Batty. Les was immune to the fundamental ground rules of the game. He would swing his conker string like Taras Bulba wielding his axe. It was absolute luck if his conker hit yours. More often than not he would strike you somewhere on your arm or chest and never say he was sorry. Should 'stringsies' occur (when the two strings wrapped around each other) he would refuse to give you an extra go. You basically let him win or suffer a further beating but this time with his fists.

Games of football, with coats as goalposts, took place in the street or on the cinder crofts throughout the year. Many a front window went through and many a backside was leathered because of it. Mrs Scanlan claimed we had her windows out more times than Hermann Göring's Dorniers.

I remember one particular day, 6 February 1958. A game of football had been scheduled in our street for after school. Lenny was to be Tommy Taylor and I was Eddie Coleman. Sandy took the role of David Pegg, Terry chose Duncan Edwards and Herbie was Mark Jones. The game never took place. Instead, people gathered together, stunned by news of the tragedy. Disbelief, numbness and shock showed on everyone's face and froze the cold air of that winter evening. This part of the city was partisan, solid red. 'United! United! United!'

The wireless had done its worst and broadcasted the Munich air disaster, and the Babes were no more. There was a change in our world of play and make belief on that sad day. Taking away many of our heroes gave us a taste of how cruel life could be. Manchester and Salford were in mourning for weeks after. It took a long time for the city's kids to move on and rebuild their lives. Finally, in the remaining weeks of Spring, and just as the Babes would have wanted, kids began to come out of this period of grief and sadness. It was, once more, refreshing to hear a knock on the front door and a young kid asking:

'Can your Ronnie come out to play?'

Being ill

MY EAR HAD BEEN THROBBING like a blind cobbler's thumb. Our family's resident physician was my gran, a retired mill girl and former employee of Alkanah Armitage's cotton mill. She seemed to be able to write a prescription for any malady, from boils to tonsillitis. Indeed, boils were her speciality, and with a swift application of a scalding hot bread poultice, a cure was instantly effected. However, the shock of receiving such a dermal incendiary was enough to make your heart stop. Sometimes, she would smear a white, slimy ointment on the abscess called sulphate of magnesium. Again, this did the trick and she would proudly proclaim, 'There y'are love, draw the bones out of a fish, that stuff will!' A far less painful way of treating a boil you would think, until she squeezed it. I saw her employ a barbaric method on my uncle Cyril's troublesome lesion involving a hot milk bottle and a darning needle – enough said. Her potion for sore throats was boiled rhubarb, as the juice obtained from this contained an organic acid that was gargled in its unsweetened form, and invariably had the prescribed effect. Salt water lavages or boiled onion juice mouthwashes were also in her repertoire for blighted throats.

My infected ear was thus within her medical capabilities. A warmed teaspoon of olive oil was poured down your ear 'ole and then plugged with a twist of cotton wool. I was next instructed to move my lower jaw up and down to assist the passage of this soothing agent. A quick massage of my ear lobe by her therapeutic fingers was then followed by a warning to keep my head to one side, making me look ridiculous when I went outside to play out with my mates. Little did I know that in forty years time I would be using olive oil again but this time to cook my bolognese sauce. Another crazy remedy of hers for sweating out a cold was to put a red-hot poker into a glass of beer and then ask you to down it in one – the beer, not the poker. I cannot recall whether or not it worked but it certainly gave me an appetite for Boddingtons many years later.

When you were really ill, you certainly knew about it. It was off to bed with a hot water bottle. Ours was made of stone and it was like getting into bed with a meteorite. It hurt when you stubbed your toe on it as you got out of bed the next morning. A fire was then lit in the bedroom's fireplace and I recall my mother bringing upstairs red-hot pieces of coal on a shovel to kick-start the blaze. Sometimes she would 'draw the fire' with a shovel and a sheet of newspaper to further accelerate the combustion process. She was, indeed, a fearless woman because the paper would often catch fire and she would grab the fireball in her hands with the dexterity of a magician, and the crushed flames would disappear. She never seemed to receive any burns using this talented manoeuvre.

Our kitchen or scullery doubled as pharmacy and triage. Pills, potions, prophylactics and unguents were all knocked out as the tater hash and tapioca were being warmed in the oven. There was a shelf on the kitchen wall that acted as a dispensary. It hosted a pair of tweezers, a bottle of J. Collis Browne mixture, gentian violet and a fine tooth-comb for nits. There were other popular additions such as a half empty bottle of kaolin and morphine left over from last month's attack of 'the runs'. Or a bottle of pink 'Opening Medicine', looking like liquid blancmange and designed to have the reverse effect. Californian Syrup of Figs too would give you a run for your money. TCP was used to treat pimples, sore throats and cuts. Its smell would announce its use on your person for hours. Iodine, a common cheap antiseptic, would stain your skin bright orange and its tincture too would also boast its presence on your skin for days. I saw Carter's Little Liver Pills being used by the population to remedy headaches, torpid liver (whatever that was), indigestion and as a laxative. Indeed, the forties and fifties seemed to be an age when people were obsessed with their bowels. Milk of Magnesia, Andrews Liver salts, Cascara were among many other preparations affecting your colon and guaranteed to 'Clear you out', as my auntie Cissie would say.

Indian Brandee was also a common addition to your domestic pharmacy. It settled your stomach by relieving colic and flatulence. This rhubarb and capsicum-containing compound was administered in warm water and my gran spiked the draught with ordinary brandy to take away its unpleasant taste. Another medicine guaranteed to make you heave was Scott's Emulsion. Indeed, just the thought of this cod liver oil preparation continues to fill me with nausea.

Many of the items dispensed by pharmacists at that time contained the addictive opiate drug morphine. The J. Collis Browne mixture contained both morphine and peppermint oil and their unique combination, known as chlorodyne, suppressed coughs and also had anti-diarrhoeal properties. A pretty good association of properties I thought – at least if you did violently cough you wouldn't need to change your trousers afterwards. Linctus codeine was yet another morphine derivative, prescribed by GPs for chesty coughs. Nowadays you can only get the drug on prescription and its dose is strictly controlled. Liquifruita was a popular alternative to such a powerful agent. I loved its taste and I would look forward to a spell of bronchitis. Camphorated Oil eased respiratory distress and was rubbed on your chest in generous quantities making you smell like a giant mothball.

Respiratory problems were not helped by smog in the winter months. This was long before the industrial clean air act was introduced and breathing through a white handkerchief would quickly reveal just how much black smoke and pollutants you were inhaling. Cold, damp evenings and still air assisted those pea soupers we all feared. Roads were seeded with galvanised oil lamps to identify junctions and roundabouts. They were also used in a feeble attempt to lift the defiant wreaths of smog. Their burning wicks seemed only to add to the carbon and soot of that dank air. This pollution would sort out the week-chested and infirm. During these appalling times the death rate would increase and select against the chronic bronchitics, asthmatics and those with pulmonary heart disease.

There was also the abundant use of mercury in various pharmaceutical preparations. Mercury had antibacterial properties and was used in several unguents and balms in the treatment of skin infections and also syphilis. No wonder there were people leaving this world with mercuric poisoning, overdosing on this toxic metal. I heard of a bloke down our street using so much mercury-based ointment on his leg ulcers that we called him the human thermometer, for he was seven foot three on a hot day and four foot five when it was cold.

Our street gang was composed of personnel who would host a strange and often alarming mixture of ailments. Laurie Horrocks had a 'lazy eye', a rather softer diagnosis than, as his unsympathetic dad would describe him, 'boss eyed'. He wore a plaster over one of the lenses of his ill-fitting NHS spectacles. The sticky dressing was always splashed with grime and curled at its edges. When he did remove his glasses one of his eyes was at right angles to the other, and appeared to have had an argument with its partner. Diane Freebody had a permanent sty on her eye and I never saw her without a generous dollop of Golden Eye Ointment pasted on her eyelid. Tony Phillips had tragically lost his mum at the age of three and he looked as though he'd never washed since that time. I'd seen 'tide marks' on necks before but his resembled a tsunami. He, like many of us, always seemed to suffer from cracked and chapped lips. My soggy balaclava constantly rubbed cold wet saliva against my lips causing them to blister. Most of my mates were skinny except for Arty Newcombe whose rotund torso and chubby legs made exercise a problem for him. He even got out of breath when he read quickly. His plump red cheeks made him look as though he was constantly blowing a trumpet. Arty's size was not helped by his apparent dependency on chip shop scratchings.

It wasn't only we humans who fell victim to pernicious diseases and ailments. Dogs too had it bad in the fifties. The number of times our gang would be in hysterics watching worm-ridden dogs drag their bottoms along a pavement in a futile attempt to curb their rectal discomfort. Kenny Amos, a nine year old from Croft Street who had protruding yellow teeth, was a very strange boy who and made it his business to throw dogs' business at people. Whilst on this unpleasant subject, I'm sure I remember some dog poo being white – or maybe it's old age bleaching my memory?

One common and dreaded infection was mumps caused by a viral attack on your salivary glands. Your symptoms were instantly recognisable since your neck and cheeks bloated with the infection. Swallowing was painful and smiling hurt. Still, there was nothing to smile about with mumps. When fat-faced Arty Newcombe suffered from mumps his face swelled that much there was no trace of any of his facial features. High temperatures accompanied earache and my mate David's mum smeared his neck in goose grease and tied one of her stockings around his head. He positively stank. Neither he nor I could understand the reason for such therapy but it seemed to do him good. Youngsters with gum boils, or tooth abscesses as they are now called, walked the streets with a knotted scarf on the tops of their heads, smelling of clove oil. Invariably, a large piece of lint cushioned the cheek next to the offending tooth. Aching teeth were savagely pulled from their gums by tying some strong cotton around the throbbing premolar. The thread was then carefully attached to a door-knob and finally, in an unceremonious manoeuvre, the door was slammed shut. Ouch!!

The advent of the NHS in 1948 came in response to the Beveridge report which recommended free healthcare to all, rich and poor, funded by National Insurance. There would be prescription medicine available for everyone. You could now visit your general practitioner without the worry of how you were going to pay for such a consultation. The days of bartering half a dozen eggs for a shot of penicillin in the bottom were over. General practice was a male-dominated profession in the fifties. However, general hospitals were staffed predominantly by females. Matron was head honcho and was in charge of everything from patient care and laundry to nurse training, cleaning and hospital food. Ward sisters terrified junior doctors and patients too, with a no nonsense approach to ward protocol. No patient could have a relapse during matron's ward round, it just made the ward look untidy. The room itself, with its shiny linoleum floor, was as long as Blackpool's prom. Doctors all wore white coats and their stethoscopes seemed to look as though they were grabbing the physician by the throat. This essential diagnostic piece of equipment was simply constructed from orange Bunsen burner tubing, but could still detect a heart murmur or lesion in the lung.

The forties was an age when killer diseases such as tuberculosis, diphtheria, polio and scarlet fever ravaged the nation. Sullied living conditions in overcrowded industrial cities proved to be a breeding ground for the agents that caused such diseases. Polio bred in dirty drains and then infected children in epidemics, usually in the summer months. Some of the worst epidemics happened in the fifties. Youngsters suddenly disappeared from classes, some never to return and some to come back in leg irons or callipers. Everyone feared the iron lung with its angled mirror above the patient's protruding head, giving its immobile resident limited contact with the back of the room. Thank heavens for the polio vaccine, first trialled in 1957. At least it can now be swallowed and not administered in a needle.

Tuberculosis, or consumption as many called this infectious killer disease, easily spread through crowded living conditions by droplet infection. One of the first television advertisements I ever saw proclaimed 'Coughs and sneezes spread diseases. Catch your germs in a handkerchief!' Pallor, weight loss and respiratory problems were the first signs of the illness. If you survived these symptoms you would be packed off to an isolation hospital or sanatorium where fresh air and a balanced diet were high on the prescription list. I recall being taken by my gran in the mid fifties to an isolation hospital in Cheshire to see my auntie Sally, who had fallen victim to TB. We could only afford to travel such a long distance twice a year and I distinctly remember me having to sit in the grounds of the hospital whilst my gran went inside. Even on cold days the hospital ward windows were open to provide the curative fresh air. All I could hear was the incessant coughing sounds of its consumptive residents. Streptomycin, a new antibiotic effective against the disease, was first used in 1944. The early diagnosis mass radiography programmes of the 1950s coupled with preventative BCG immunisation soon reduced the number of deaths from the disease.

A lad two streets away fell into the River Irwell near Soapy Tom's soap works and died from diphtheria. This tragedy terrified the life out of us kids because we would frequently play on the river's banks and dive in during warm summer weeks. His brother would gather small crowds of nine-year olds around him and describe, in gruesome detail, the way his brother was choked to death by the disease. That same lad went on to be an undertaker in Bury.

Scarlet fever is another illness you do not hear much about these days. It too was an alarming debility causing fever and a bright red rash on the chest that soon spread over the body. It could lead to rheumatic fever, another unpleasant condition, often causing heart valve disease later in life.

Today's battle with obesity certainly did not feature in the forties and fifties. A Big Mac was something your dad wore when it was chucking it down, and pizza, wasn't that something to do with a leaning tower? However, malnutrition did exist for many of us who lacked the essential balanced diet. Five a day was impossible. In Salford, local health clinics ran sun ray treatment sessions for primary school kids to give them the necessary vitamin D. The weekly irradiation meant you being forced to wear perished and cracked rubber goggles that stank and pinched your skin. The only plus for enduring the twenty minutes was to be given a glass of orange juice, followed by a teaspoon of malt. Some weeks the recipe would change and it was a spoon of cod liver oil that would make us all heave.

The days prior to the Clean Air Act of 1958 saw the city enveloped in wreaths of smoke from factories in Trafford Park and Greengate and Irwell. This prevented the sun's rays from hitting our skin, leading to rickets. I knew at least two kids in neighbouring streets who suffered from this bone-softening disorder. Alec Mason possessed a pair of lower limbs that described a circle and he was a terrible school goalkeeper.

Perhaps I became immune to noticing the number of people with limps. They seemed de rigueur for old blokes. It was a cruel practice for us kids to tease Mr Broadbent, the Peel Park parky. We would shout quite insulting remarks at him and then laugh out loud when he tried to chase us, waddling like an arthritic duck, shaking his fist and shouting 'I'll give ya "gammy leg" when I catch ya little buggers!'

In your primary school class there were usually a couple of pigeon-chested asthmatics that would be bundled out of the classroom by an alarmed teacher when they were having an attack. Paul Eason used to go yellow, green and then blue during his shortness of breath episodes. Lyndsay Waters was constantly scratching because of bed bug bites, her arms and legs daubed in gentian violet. She lived in Rossall Street and in the summer months you could smell the bugs when you stood at the top of the street. Sean O'Leary stank of the mustard plasters used by his mother to ward off chest infections. Occasionally some poor soul carried an oatmeal poultice to remedy poison ivy. Horace Beeney's hair contained more life than Noah's Ark and he was always being pulled out of our class by the nit nurse. His mother would bend his head forward over a sheet of newspaper then drag a fine metal tooth comb through his hair. You could hear and see the nits fall onto the paper with each stroke of the comb.

During the weeks of August some youngsters would go on their holidays to Blackpool, Southport or Morecambe. They would return resembling a human plaster cast, smothered in dried calamine lotion to ease their sunburn. Skin temperatures were achieved on which you could turn steak from rare to well done. Next, the phenomenon of peeling would take place on the grand scale. Patches of loose, dry skin would flake in layers giving the person a rather alarming appearance, almost as though you were rotting away. Horace, on his return from the poor kids of Salford camp in Blackpool, once resembled an insect shedding its skin. Unfortunately, he would do himself no favours in terms of making friends as he insisted on scratching his dry skin flakes as you were eating your packet of Smiths Crisps.

The fifties was an era when new antibiotics were used for a wide range of bacterial infections. Aspirin was, and of course still is, a great drug used to soothe pain and reduce temperature. Perhaps the most striking piece of scientific research undertaken at this time was that establishing a link between smoking and lung cancer. As a kid, it seemed nearly everyone smoked. Film stars with huge followings such as Humphrey Bogart and Lauren Bacall seemed to make it fashionable and legitimise the habit. I remember seeing the film 'The Maltese Falcon', where each character smoked incessantly. The on-screen activities of these cinema greats were conducted against a constant veil of white mist. I believe the falcon itself was on forty a day. The research and its implications were slow to persuade the public, and sadly today many people still fail to heed this sixty-year old discovery.

The late fifties was an age that saw huge advances in medical science. Yes, ice cream was still prescribed by nurses following your painful tonsillectomy, but new ground was broken in both preventative medicine and surgery. The first kidney transplant took place in 1954 and this new concept of transplantation paved the way for more life-saving, complex surgery in the 1960s.

Butlin's by the sea: a girl's tale

Zip-A-Dee-Doo-Dah,
Zip-A-Dee-A
My o' my what a wonderful day!
Plenty of sunshine heading our way
Zip-A-Dee-Doo-Dah,
Zip-A-Dee-A!

THIS WAS THE LAST TIME a reveille of such hideous nature would punch its way through the morning air. The camp public address speakers vibrated with this Disney ditty, denoting the start of a new day. Indeed, it was my final few hours at this holiday wonderland. I didn't want to go home, nor did my brother and sister. It was over, all bar the breakfast.

Seven days earlier my family had arrived for a week's full board at Butlin's, Pwllheli. You couldn't do anything else but book full board; all of your worries taken care of by this multi-million pound organisation. The charabanc, or chara as we called it, dropped us off at the gates. Everything seemed so colourful and inviting. Neatly trimmed lawns hosted flowerbeds teaming with blooms. An avenue of flags, fluttering on top of white-painted flagpoles, drew you down towards the reception area, where a huge sign said 'Welcome To Butlin's'.

Pwllheli, on the North Wales coast was noted for its sea breezes and bracing air. During our week's stay here I never once witnessed the flags hanging still.

'It'll blow the cobwebs off yer!' shouted my dad as he wrestled with our suitcases, both of which were cleverly reinforced by one of his old belts.

At the reception hall we were welcomed by a group of Redcoats. The male hosts wore white shoes, white flannels and shirt. Their shirt collars were folded over the lapels of their post-box red blazers. The female Redcoats sported white plimsolls and socks. Their skirt, again, was jet white with pleats all round and finished three inches below the knee. My little brother Lawrence seemed entranced by the number of badges they wore on these jackets. On the top pocket of their blazers was the Butlin's logo of the entwined letters BHC.

We too were given a Butlin's badge, a metal one with the words 'Butlin's Pwllheli', and told we must wear it at all times, particularly if we journeyed out of the camp. My brother, anxious to increase his own badge collection, immediately signed up as a Butlin's Beaver. There was a Beaver code of conduct and my mum was pessimistic about him upholding such righteous behaviour, mainly because he still had a black eye from a recent fight in our street over a game of marbles.

Every camper was allocated a House, of which there were six. A small pamphlet explained the importance of the House system. Not only was it supposed to encourage an *esprit de corps* in the competitions arranged for the week but also sort out logistical arrangements for meals. I remember feeling proud of belonging to Connaught House and I would eagerly participate in the playful derision of rival House members.

Our chalet was a mid terrace, like back home, so no change there then. Bunk beds for us made going to bed an exciting prospect. Our own wash basin in the room made us feel incredibly middle class.

'Blimey!' said dad, 'you can hardly swing a cat round here.' As kids, we could never understand why he always used cat swinging as a measure of volume. What on earth was he moaning at? It was wonderful to us. Immediately outside our block was a patch of lawn separating us from the chalets opposite. We'd never had a lawn before. Animated kids were running up and down, some in their swimming costumes, others carrying beach balls and tennis rackets. We wanted to be part of this frenzied activity as quickly as possible.

'Go and take 'em for an explore, Walter, while I unpack and get straight,' shouted my mum as she started to open the suitcases.

Butlin's radio belted out an itinerary for the evening and told you to consult your programme for the week. This information was usually preceded by an annoying jingle:

'Butlin's! Butlin's! Butlin's by the sea.
Have fun when you want to. Be as
gay as you want to.
At Butlin's by the sea!'

This is an encouraging message for today's Equal Opportunities Commission, I am sure, but in those days this frequent memorandum was quite irritating.

Inter-House competitions such as football, swimming, tug of war, obstacle races and rounders were interspersed with glamorous granny competitions, best physique and fancy dress. My dad came second in the 'Knobbly Knees' show. I thought the Redcoat in charge was rather harsh on dad when he described his legs as hairy celery. I have never witnessed so many varicose veins. One contestant's legs looked like the wiring of the National Grid. It took three pints of beer, consumed at the Pig and Whistle bar, for both him and the father from the family in the next chalet to us, to have the resolve to enter this lower limb challenge.

The Kershaws were a family from Kirby in Liverpool. Indeed, the camp seemed to be overrun with Scousers, the air being saturated with mutant words like 'dat', 'dis', 'bachh' and 'cum ed la'. My dad would always say of Scousers 'They'd pinch yer teeth and come back for yer gums.' I never heard him mention this demographic stereotype to Mr Kershaw though, who was now his new drinking buddy.

Parents would always put on their best clothes for their evening's entertainment that often included a visit to the Viennese Bar or the camp theatre. Nannies dressed as nursing extras from 'Emergency Ward Ten' patrolled the rows of chalets and listened for babies crying. Information was then relayed to parents via flashing signs in the ballroom, cinema and pubs: 'Baby crying in chalet D7'

Abandoning children in chalets was perfectly acceptable in the fifties and nobody was reported to social services and the child protection team. Similarly, the staff looking after your children in the tiny tots corner or nursery rhyme land, though dressed in quasi NHS apparel, were free from today's CRB scrutiny.

There was entertainment for all at this wonderful place. Punch and Judy, the paddling pool with its tiered fountain and the kiddies' playground catered for one end of the age spectrum. Children returned from their Butlin's experience addicted to table tennis. Billiards, ballroom dancing, well-stocked bars and cabaret seemed to satisfy the more senior fringe. Redcoats worked extremely hard organising shows, games and quizzes. Some were excellent singers and dancers whilst others simply made you laugh. I had a crush on a Redcoat named Tony who came from Hull. He had a lovely smile and always called me gorgeous. I did go off him though when I saw him frenziedly picking his nose near the pitch and putt kiosk.

Teenage girls aspired to be Miss Butlin, Pwllheli, and spotty male youths wearing cheap suits and winkle picker shoes strived to be 'The Best Dressed Male'. I witnessed a limbo dancing competition in the ballroom on one Wednesday evening. A man in his early twenties won the event but was later disqualified for tying casters to his knees under his trousers. This Caribbean evening was a great success and introduced the mild and bitter swigging populations of Merseyside and Manchester to rum punch and banana daiquiris. One parochial soul from St Helens, when asked by Tony the Redcoat had he ever heard of sweet potato, replied 'Is it chips with sugar on?' This spirit of competition kept everyone busy and, supposedly, enjoying themselves.

The camp field and large open air swimming pool were centres for more competitive events. Lines of people from the six Houses would pass medicine balls between their legs then over their heads. Each line contained contestants who were deadly serious along with others who just laughed their way through the proceedings. In the pool, hopping races alternated with relays. Obstacle courses made from lorry tyre inner-tubes, large plastic ducks and lilos would keep everyone amused, even those who nearly drowned in the process.

Early morning keep fit classes were attended by a few of the campers, collectively known as 'nutters' by their fellow holidaymakers.

'They're a load of physical jerks,' quipped my dad, who was about as athletic as Bessie Braddock. The Redcoat in charge of such strenuous activity would dress in white shorts, plimsolls and a white vest. He seemed to relish pain and torture. His blonde hair and clean cut, lean appearance would have made him ideal for the Hitler Youth.

Adding to the charm of the site was a lake and a miniature railway. You could also hire curiously constructed bicycles, so-called pedal cars, that were really two machines welded together and the riders sat side by side. Camp speed limits were constantly ignored by adolescent hell-raisers as they tore around the tarmac.

An important part of the Butlin manifesto was that good food makes a good holiday. The three meals per day were served up in a huge dining hall the size of Maine Road. These premises seated over one thousand diners and sittings were according to Houses. Mealtimes were not only a gourmet experience but also a mechanism for announcing competition results, collating House points and whipping up enthusiasm and hysteria for future tournaments. Cheers and applause would garnish your meat and three veg as Mavis Batty of Gloucester House was announced as winner of today's Donkey Derby. Cheers too rang through the dining chamber as plates tumbled to the floor, dropped by speeding waiters, moving between rows of tables.

Most of the serving staff were pleasant enough, though I remember one waiter whose redolent Park Drive breath was accompanied by an attitude akin to Cesare Borgia.

A waitress would serve you breakfast with fresh love bites on her neck following an evening liaison with a vampire kitchen hand who had proclaimed his undying love for her the night before. Soup was the starter for every evening meal and was often served to your table either with or without a thumb. 'Afters' was often jam roly-poly and custard or ice cream and a wafer. If you were one of those new breeds called vegetarians then it was hard luck; just give the meat to someone else on your table. Should you be vegan then funeral arrangements were quickly made.

Another optional task, but deemed mandatory by some of your House Redcoats, was to complete cards with the names and addresses of friends for Butlin's promotions to contact. A prize was given at the end of the week for the greatest number of referrals. I started to invent people in my desperate attempt to win a cut-price holiday deal for next year.

My mother was obsessed with knitting and much of the day she spent looking after us in the play areas or on the field. At four o'clock each day she would get a chair outside the chalet and proceed to knit for England. On days that it rained she would walk to a room called 'the quiet area' and complete twelve blankets there whilst other people wrote postcards home proclaiming 'Wish you were here!' Or, if it were addressed to my Auntie Cissie, my dad would shout to my mother, 'Put glad you're NOT here, Ethel!' These postcards usually arrived at their destination a good week after you'd been home.

The final evening meal in the dining hall was always special. Families who had become friends swapped addresses and promises were made. Trophies were given to House champions and prizes dished out by the same team of assiduous Redcoats. I couldn't believe it when my name was shouted out as the person who had completed the greatest number of referral cards. To tumultuous applause I walked to the podium and there stood Redcoat Tony holding a white envelope containing a half price holiday for us next year. He bent down and kissed me on the cheek and simultaneously pushed the gift into my hands.

'There y'are gorgeous,' he whispered, convinced he was the most attractive male on the planet.

I suppose my reflex response to such flattery should have been to blush, swoon and become quite emotional. However, all I could think about was that I hoped he'd washed his hands.

Food, glorious food

FOOD RATIONING FOR THE NATION finally ended in July 1954. A year earlier, because of the coronation, every family was awarded an extra pound of sugar and four ounces of margarine – ideal if you made cakes but not if you hadn't seen a lamb chop for years. You would have to wait another twelve months for meat and cheese to come off the ration book. So, delicacies such as spam fritters, corned beef or tata hash and powdered egg comprised the main meat or protein component of people's diet until the end of rationing. Kids who lived in more rural areas outside Manchester and Salford were paid sixpence by a butcher for snaring a rabbit, and two bob for a hare. Horse meat was not uncommon and my uncle Tommy, having returned from the Malaya campaign a few years earlier, would moan, 'I've had so much horse meat that if someone cracks a whip, I'm off at a gallop!'

Remember, this was an age of make do and mend. It was also an age when we championed Lancashire hotpot. The amount of lamb it contained varied as to how much you could afford, or who you knew. People who dined on tinned peaches soaked in ideal milk had aspirations above their station. Mums would purchase a bag of broken biscuits and still retain their dignity. As kids we would shout to the grocer Eddie O'Driscoll, 'Have you got any broken biscuits, Eddie?' Eddie would then nod to confirm he had. Our witty reply was, 'Well, mend 'em!' and then leg it quick. Was this paediatric alternative comedy?

Today's healthy eating principle of five a day could never have operated during these austere times. Vegetables were potatoes, cabbage, swede, carrots and peas. Aubergine was a colour spoken about by the bourgeoisie, and chilli was a synonym for cold. I never saw broccoli until I was nineteen and spinach was in tins eaten by Popeye. Yoghurt was sour milk and we had plenty of that. Everything was seasonal. Consequently, if you fancied a salad in January, well, that was hard cheese. It probably was hard cheese too because nobody had refrigerators and nothing was vacuum packed or even wrapped. Good, wholesome and healthy food provided you with the energy needed to get you through the day and stuck to yer ribs as my granddad would say. Indeed, every meat dish that needed frying was done in beef lard or dripping. Oil was solely for your bicycle chain or a Singer sewing machine. An uncle of mine, who my mother would describe as being 'slow up top' – an affectionate term which reflected the man's simplicity – would poke his head around the butcher's shop door and shout, 'Oy, Ossie, do ya keep dripping?' The butcher would reply, 'Yes, 'course I do!' to which my asinine relative would shout, 'So do I. It's embarrassing i'nt it!'

In chip shops, battered fish was fried in this fat. People ate fish on Fridays. A penneth of scratchings moved your cholesterol levels off the scale. The taste, however, has never been equalled and people would say it was a taste to die for. A cardiologist friend of mine modified that sentence stating that it was a taste to die from. Fish and chips were excellent value for money; you got an energy-giving meal and the newspaper in which they were wrapped gave you a good read as well. Nowadays we have some Chinese chippies, but back then I knew of only one, Kim Ling Po, a joiner from Broughton. Fried bread done in lard was a sumptuous taste and provided you with enough energy to climb the Matterhorn.

Chip shops were the only real examples of takeaway food emporia. Indeed, if you'd have asked a little lad from Eccles what a takeaway was he would have replied that it was a hard sum and the opposite of adding up – also a hard sum. You had to journey into Manchester if you fancied anything exotic to eat. By the term exotic I mean the food was served on fancy plates and your cup of tea was brought to you with sugar cubes – posh! I think there was only one Chinese restaurant in the city at that time. Indian restaurants were found near the river

Ganges, thousands of miles from the river Irwell. The term naan was reserved for your granny. Mint and parsley were the only two herbs used in cooking. Most people believed basil was a posh bloke's name and sage was a wise man. Garlic was never found in any greengrocer's shop. Jam butties filled you up and the energy hit from sugar butties made you hyperactive.

People mainly drank tea in those days. It quenched your thirst and its leaves told your fortune at the same time. If anyone had told me that in fifty years hence I would pay one pound for a small bottle of water, I'd have had them sectioned under the Mental Health Act. Camp coffee was a liquid coffee concentrate that had the unmistakable picture of a Scottish Highlander on its label. Someone bought us a bottle of the stuff but it gathered dust in our pantry, my gran saying, 'Tastes like strychnine, I don't hold with the stuff!'

There was something refreshing about a cup of Typhoo poured from the teapot. Invariably teapots had a tea cosy, knitted by a well-meaning relative. The tea cosy was our first attempt at conserving heat energy and paved the way for cavity wall and loft insulation. Remember, pipes frequently burst in our cold winters, and old socks and pullovers were wrapped around the lead pipework in your outside loo. The winter of 1951 was a great time for plumbers, and the number of bulging, sweated lead joints was testimony to over ninety days of snow. I also heard of some enterprising soul in October 1956 attempting to sell sheets of honeycomb tripe as carpet underlay. Sadly, his business closed in November 1956.

There was always joy and excitement when you were invited to someone's birthday party. Sandwich triangles of chicken paste or fish spread were the main carbohydrate component of the menu. This was always followed by jelly and blancmange and sometimes pineapple chunks with carnation milk. We all guzzled 'pop' supplied by the Corona man, whose fine vintages of cream soda or dandelion and burdock schmoozed out taste buds. The fizzy drinks forced the boys to have burping contests while the girls looked on disgusted with their antics, except Janice Garside – a large-chested girl who could burp like a gurgling drain. The empty pop bottle, which had a tuppence redemption fee, was often used to play spin the bottle, whereby boys had to kiss girls – outrageous, and the start of the permissive society! Party bags containing flying saucers, spangles, dolly mixtures, love hearts and penny Spanish all played their role in dental caries. Invariably, someone would overdose on pop and sweeties and be sick in the back yard, practising for our future binge society. The name coke in those days meant nothing to youngsters, but to parents it was fuel for the fire.

Christmas time saw the purchase of foods we never ate during the rest of the year. Families were to see bananas, tangerines, pomegranates and coconuts for the first time. Brazil nuts were impossible to crack. Walnuts and almonds were easier and that cretin of an uncle of mine would crack them with his teeth – some people in evolution advance less quickly than others!

A packet of dates always emerged some time during the Christmas celebrations and gave you sticky fingers for hours. My auntie used to complain their skins always got under her teeth and she was frequently seen washing her falsies under the kitchen tap just when my mother was dishing up Christmas dinner – charming! Christmas dinner was chicken in most urban areas and as far as us street kids knew, turkeys, capons and geese were found in Belle Vue Zoo.

At other festive periods such as Shrove Tuesday it was pancakes for all. Indeed, if you didn't like pancakes then you didn't get much to eat on that day. It was great fun helping your mum prepare the mixture, putting measures of the mix into the pan and then hurling the congealed mass into the air. Many a kitchen ceiling still bore the egg and flour scars from last year's uncoordinated efforts. Pancakes had kilograms of sugar sprinkled over them. The calorific experience of these delicacies was then intensified as some over zealous kid smeared jam over this already sweetened galette. I never got on with lemons after Kenny Bagnall, a huge fifteen-year old bully from a street nearby, made me and my mate Herbie suck two lemons each whilst pinning us against the wall. My salivary glands to this day have never quite recovered. At Easter you ate hot cross buns that were only available in shops days before Good Friday and were sold out by Easter Monday, never to be baked again for another year.

It is now fashionable to dine al fresco. It sometimes happened in the fifties in streets situated in rough areas of Salford. However, tables and chairs on the pavement usually signified eviction. The closest we ever got to dining outside was a picnic in the park where we would take a tablecloth, vacuum flask and biscuits. Ginger nuts, custard creams and garibaldi biscuits were our favourites, though I did put my cousin off the garibaldi when I called them fly cemeteries.

The difficult thing with perishable foods in those days was stopping them 'going off'. Refrigeration was in its infancy and families had to find ways of preventing this food spoilage. Some people had meat safes that had a metallic gauze grille in the door where cuts of meat and cheese were stored outside in the shade. Milk could be kept in a bucket of cold water with a damp tea towel over the top. Water from the wet towel would evaporate and cool the air inside. The Andersons next door to us had raised one of the flagstones in the back yard, dug a pit, put the milk bottle into the hole, and then replaced the stone. Milk could be bought as sterilised but it was a taste not liked by all. I recall my mother boiling milk that was just about to go on the turn to get a couple of extra days' mileage out of it. Conversely in the winter, a bottle of milk on your doorstep would freeze and a column of frozen milk would rise out of the bottle and raise the silver cap a good couple of inches. Full cream milk in those days allowed you to see exactly how much cream you were getting as it separated out at the top inside the bottle. A lady in our street would hang curdled milk in a nylon stocking over the back of a chair, allowing the whey to drip into a bowl below. When the curds had dried, she'd add a pinch of salt and there was the cheese for her husband's sandwiches.

We will all remember school dinners. You got your meat and two veg in some form or other. Invariably the vegetable component was cabbage and swede. Whoever was in charge of mashing at the council kitchens where these gourmet delights were prepared could have done with taking a course of pumping iron with Charles Atlas. Lumpy spuds and hard cubes of swede made lunchtime dining 'al dente', and quite an unpleasant experience. Occasionally you would be served macaroni cheese or steamed fish. The high spot of such fine alimentation was pudding or afters, usually some form of milk pudding such as rice, semolina or tapioca and dotted with a blob of jam to make it more appetising. The smell and the slightest taste of semolina would make me heave. I was more of a jam or golden syrup sponge and custard person. Morris Benson fed like a frenzied hyena. He polished off everyone's leftovers and always chewed his food with his mouth open. It was like staring into a cement mixer and he was always first in the queue for seconds. Morris was, however, as skinny as a pipe cleaner because he had the metabolism of a jet engine.

I do not miss feeling hungry, nor do I miss not having any money in my pocket. I do, however, miss that addictive smell of my mother's freshly baked bread. I long for hotpot with beetroot and red cabbage. I sometimes recall gnawing away at jellied pigs' trotters dashed with salt and vinegar giving that extra piquancy. I regularly import black puddings from the Bury Market Pudding Company. These pigs' blood and oatmeal parcels boost my iron levels so much that on rainy days I suffer from rust. I now eat muesli that I would once have described as cattle feed but I am still disappointed to find there's no novelty inside. I now buy baguettes and no longer think they are small bags. I do miss the little blue bag of salt in packets of Smith's Crisps. On occasions, I am reminded of Monday's mouth-watering sandwich of bread and dripping. I recall sucking a Jubbly until my lips froze to its icy surface. I do miss the taste of haslet and brawn. Sadly, savoury ducks, cowheel and elder no longer feature on our weekly menus.

I am indebted to my mother and gran for putting food on the table in such hard times. However, two things you would never find on their table were bad manners and elbows!

A postscript

I AM INDEBTED TO JOAN, *a member of Salford Local History Society. This sagacious lady reminded me that it was Police Street Clinic where schoolchildren had to journey for their sun-ray treatment to boost their Vitamin D levels, warding off rickets. It was also the venue for inspections by the nit nurse, Nitty Nora, as the older children would call her.*

My very first day at school saw a visit from her. The Headteacher came into our class and told us five-year olds to line up outside the school office. We obediently shuffled along the long corridor and stood, in single file outside this room. I quickly became aware that a rather corpulent lady, clad in a dark blue uniform, was moving from one person to another, rummaging through their hair. The lady looked like a female version of Friar Tuck except that she had a full head of hair resembling a burst spring interior. None of us had been told the reason for such an examination. Anxious to understand the purpose of this procedure I turned to the boy behind me and enquired if he knew what this lady was doing. The knowledgeable urchin replied,

'I think she's checkin' if you've got any brains!'

It was now my turn to stand below this beefy agent of preventative medicine. She then ransacked my golden curls and shouted down to me.

'Right. Go back to yer class. You haven't got any!'

So, there you have it. From day one at primary school, I was stigmatised as a numpty and I have shouldered that diagnosis all my life. God bless the NHS.